SPELLING WORKOUT

Phillip K. Trocki

Modern Curriculum Press

EXECUTIVE EDITOR	Wendy Whitnah
PROJECT EDITOR	Diane Dzamtovski
EDITORIAL DEVELOPMENT DESIGN AND PRODUCTION	The Hampton-Brown Company
ILLUSTRATORS	Anthony Accardo, Joe Boddy, Roberta Collier-Morales, Sandra Forrest, Carlos Freire, Ron Grauer, Meryl Henderson, Jane McCreary, Yoshi Miyake, Masami Miyamoto, Deborah Morse, Doug Roy, John Sandford, Rosalind Solomon.
PHOTO CREDITS	25, Comstock; 57, Carlos Valdes-Dapena/Comstock; 60, Thomas Wear/Comstock; 61, Roberta Hershenson/Photo Researchers; 62, Henry Georgi/Comstock; 63, Bob Daemmrich/Uniphoto; 64, Barbara Rios/Photo Researchers; 89, J. Carmichael Jr./Image Bank; 00, J.H. Robinson/Animals Animals; 125, Robert A. Lubeck/Earth Scenes; 133, Sobol/Sipa Press; 141, John P. Kelly/Image Bank.
COVER DESIGN	The Hampton-Brown Company
COVER PHOTO	Steve Satushek/Image Bank

Typefaces for the manuscript type in this book were provided by Zaner-Bloser, Inc., Columbus, Ohio, copyright, 1993.

MODERN CURRICULUM PRESS

An Imprint of Pearson Learning
299 Jefferson Road, P.O. Box 480
Parsippany, N.J. 07054-0480
http://www.mcschool.com

ISBN 0-8136-2815-6

9 10 11 12 13 14 15   02 01 00 99

TABLE OF CONTENTS

Learning to Spell a Word

1. Say the word.
   Look at the word and say the letters.

2. Print the word with your finger.

3. Close your eyes and think of the word.

4. Cover the word and print it on paper.

5. Check your spelling.

6. Write your spelling words in your Spelling Notebook at the back of your book.

Beginning and Ending Sounds

Say the names of the pictures in each box.
Which ones have the same **beginning** sound?
Draw a line to connect the pictures with the
same **beginning** sound.

Say the names of the pictures in each
box. Which ones have the same **ending**
sound? Draw a line to connect the
pictures with the same **ending** sound.

Say the name of the first picture in the row. Circle each picture in the row with the same **beginning** sound as the first picture.

Say the name of the first picture in the row. Circle each picture in the row with the same **beginning** sound as the first picture.

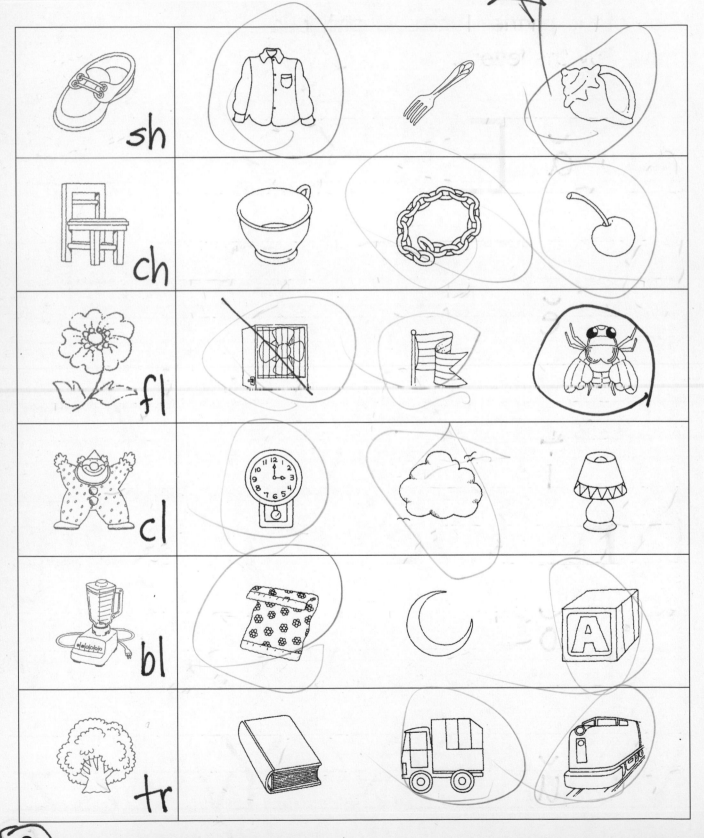

Alphabet Review

Look at the partner letters, capital and small. Say the letters.

Aa Bb Cc

Dd Ee Ff Gg Hh

Ii Jj Kk Ll Mm

Nn Oo Pp Qq

Rr Ss Tt Uu Vv

Ww Xx Yy Zz

Look at the letter in the circle. Then circle
the letter that is just like it at the right.

Ⓔ	F	E	T
Ⓚ	z	x	K
ⓜ	h	n	m
Ⓢ	b	S	J
Ⓠ	O	q	Q
ⓓ	B	d	b
Ⓘ	I	i	T
ⓐ	d	a	c
Ⓑ	B	D	d
Ⓥ	M	Y	V

Ⓛ	T	L	I
ⓕ	f	F	j
Ⓖ	Q	C	G
ⓗ	u	n	h
Ⓤ	v	U	h
ⓒ	u	c	o
Ⓙ	U	j	J
Ⓝ	N	W	V
Ⓡ	P	R	B
ⓣ	T	I	t

Say the alphabet. Fill in the missing
capital letters.

Look at the capital letter. Circle its small partner letter.

Look at the small letter. Circle its capital partner letter.

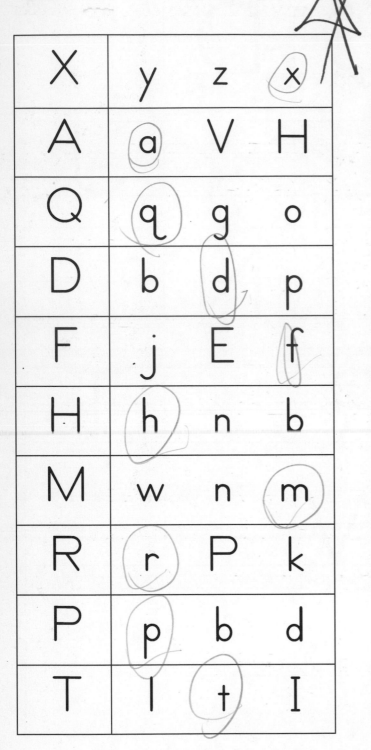

X	y	z	x
A	a	V	H
Q	q	g	o
D	b	d	p
F	j	E	f
H	h	n	b
M	w	n	m
R	r	P	k
P	p	b	d
T	l	t	I

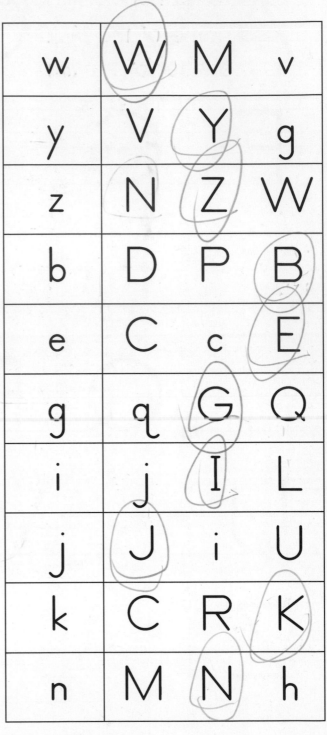

w	W	M	v
y	V	Y	g
z	N	Z	W
b	D	P	B
e	C	c	E
g	q	G	Q
i	j	I	L
j	J	i	U
k	C	R	K
n	M	N	h

Name _____

Sounds and Letters A–N

Say the name of the picture.
Trace the letter of the first sound.   Write 3
Then print the letter.

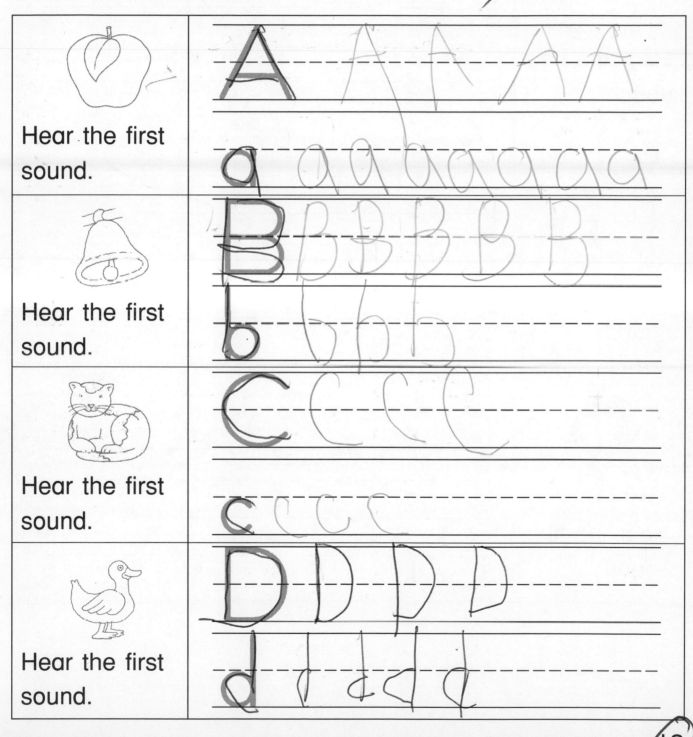

Hear the first sound.

Hear the first sound.

Hear the first sound.

Hear the first sound.

13

Say the name of the picture.
Trace the letter of the first sound.
Then print the letter.

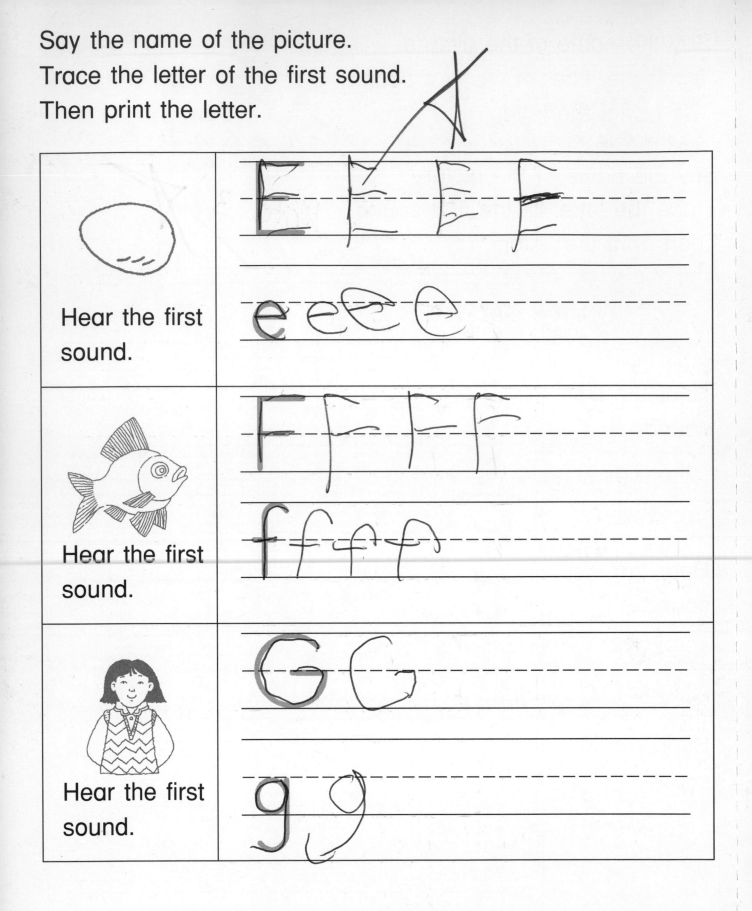

Hear the first sound.

Hear the first sound.

Hear the first sound.

Say the name of the picture.
Trace the letter of the first sound.
Then print the letter.

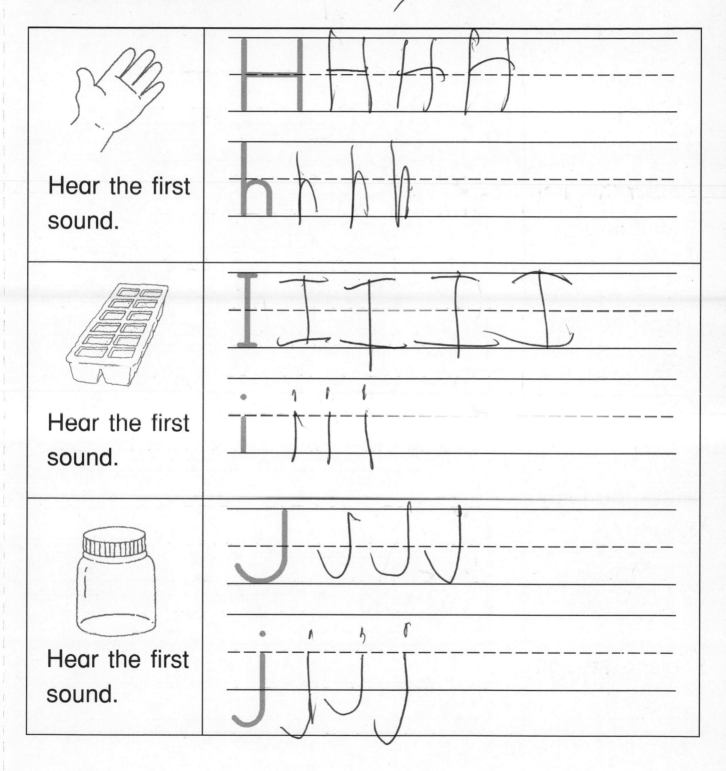

Hear the first sound.

Hear the first sound.

Hear the first sound.

Say the name of the picture.
Trace the letter of the first sound.
Then print the letter.

Hear the first sound.

Hear the first sound.

Hear the first sound.

Hear the first sound.

Name _____

Sounds and Letters O–Z

Say the name of the picture.
Trace the letter of the first sound.
Then print the letter.

Hear the first sound.

Hear the first sound.

Hear the first sound.

Say the name of the picture.
Trace the letter of the first sound.
Then print the letter.

Hear the first sound.

R R R R
r r r r r

Hear the first sound.

S S S S
s s s s

Hear the first sound.

T T T T
t t t t

Say the name of the picture.
Trace the letter of the first sound.
Then print the letter.

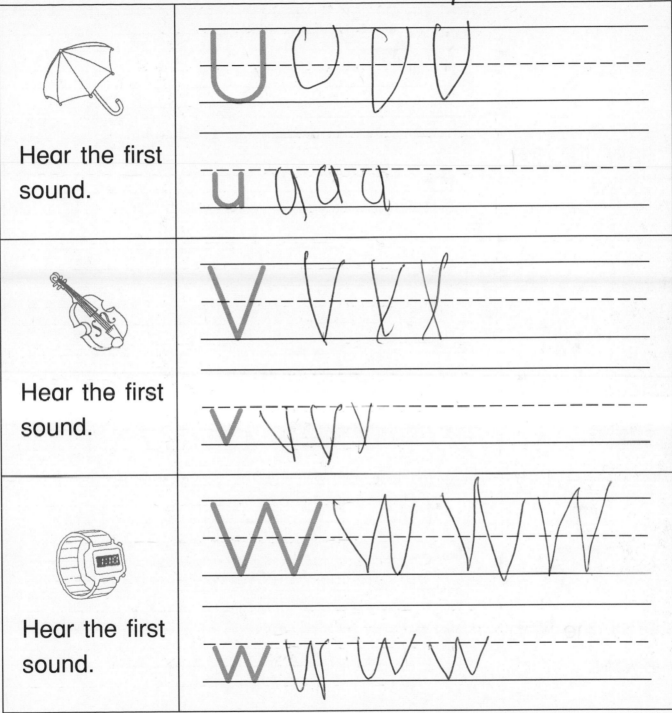

Hear the first sound.

Hear the first sound.

Hear the first sound.

Say the name of the picture.
Trace the letter of the sound.
Then print the letter.

Hear the **last** sound.

Hear the first sound.

Hear the first sound.

Name _____

Matching Sounds and Letters

Say the name of each picture.
How does each start? Circle the letter
that stands for the beginning sound.

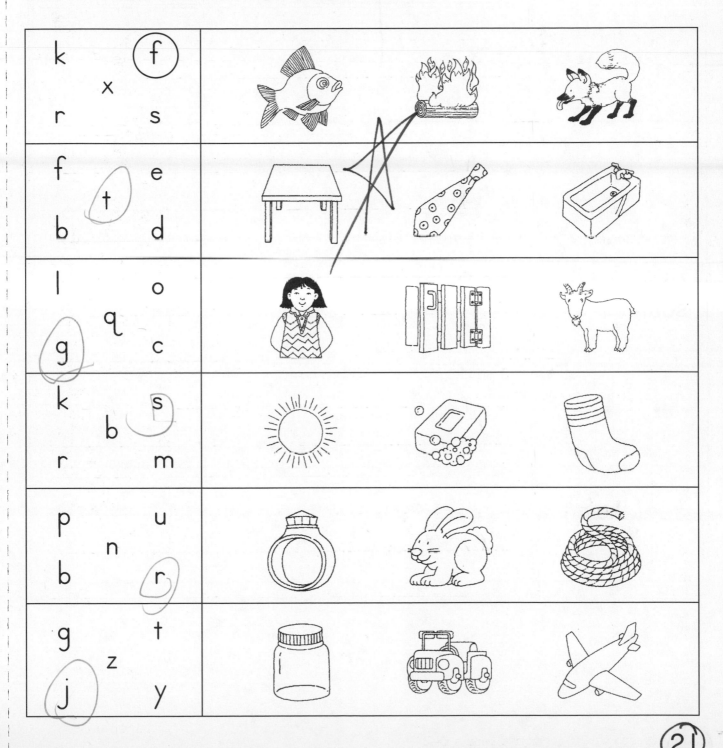

k (f) x r s	fish	fire	fox
f e (t) b d	table	tie	tub
l o q c (g)	girl	case	goat
k (s) b r m	sun	soap	sock
p u n b (r)	ring	rabbit	rope
g t z (j) y	jar	truck	plane

Say the name of each picture.
How does each end? Circle the letter
that stands for the <u>ending</u> sound.

				(r)	d
				a	
				s	c
				m	l
				(k)	d
					h
				i	(n)
				f	h
					p
				b	r
				(d)	
				l	c
				(g)	w
					d
				p	b
				w	n
					r
				h	(m)

Say the name of each picture in the box. How does it start? Draw a line to connect the picture with the letter that stands for its beginning sound.

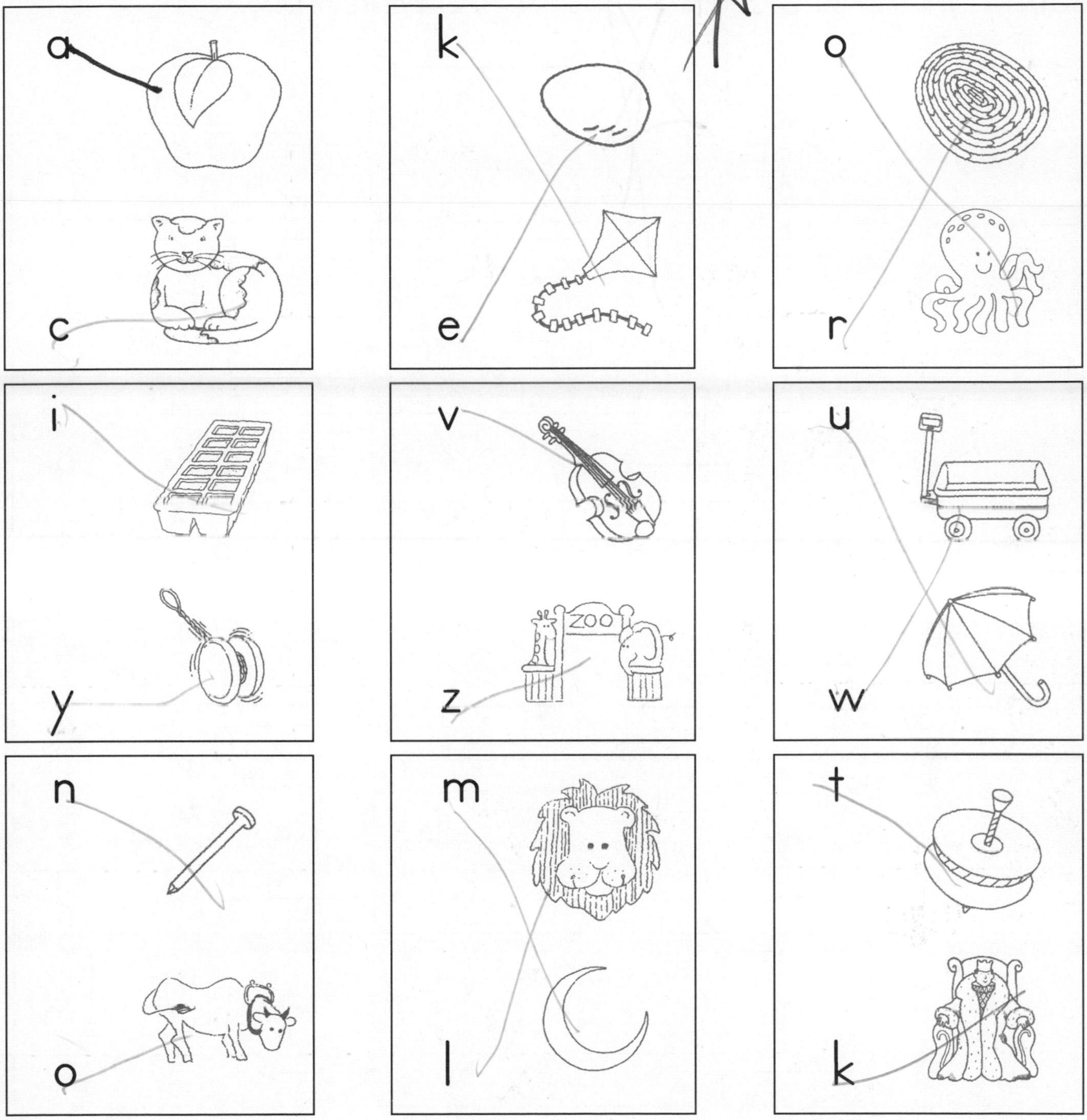

a

c

k

e

o

r

i

y

v

z

u

w

n

o

m

l

t

k

Say the name of each picture. How does it start? Circle the letter. Print the letter of the beginning sound on the line.

Say the name of each picture. How does it end? Circle the letter. Print the letter of the ending sound on the line.

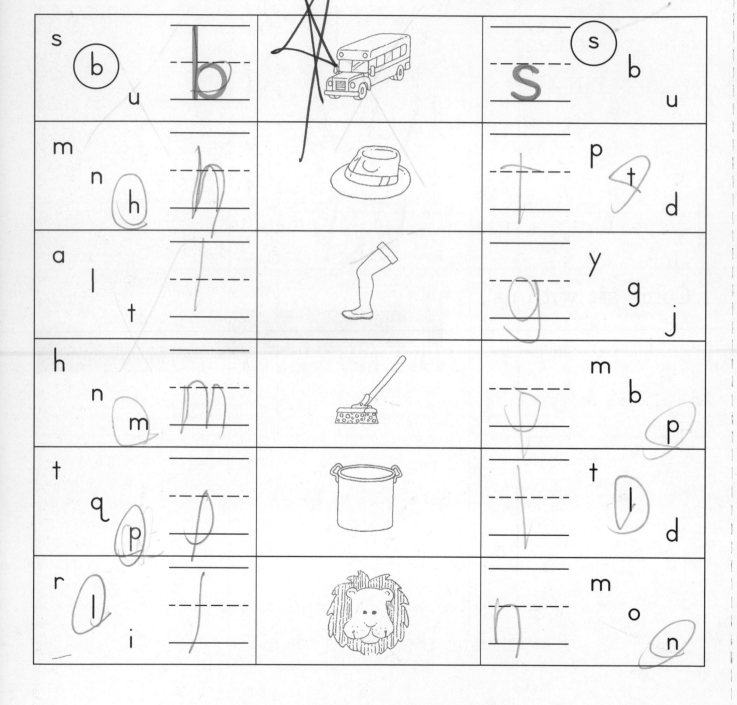

Lesson 5 ■ Matching Sounds and Letters

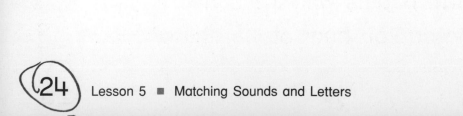

Beginning and Ending <u>s</u>, <u>t</u>, <u>b</u>

Get Ready

Read the sentences.

Hello! Hello!
We **see** the **bus.**
Hello! Hello!
Can the bus see us?
Wave. Make a fuss!
Here.
Come **sit** with us!

Get Set

Read the sentences again. Say each word in dark print. Listen for the beginning and the ending sounds.

 The word **sit** begins with the sound for **s.**
It ends with the sound for **t.**

 The word **bus** begins with the sound for **b.**
It ends with the sound for **s.**

 The word **tub** begins with the sound for **t.**
What sound do you hear at the end of **tub?**

Go!

Sounds, Letters, and Words

Look at the pictures. Print the letter that stands for the missing beginning sound or ending sound. Trace the letters to spell List Words.

LIST WORDS

1. tub
2. bus
3. bat
4. see
5. sit
6. us

1. _____ us

2. _____ si

3. _____ tu

4. _____ at

5. _____ ee

6. _____ u

Beginning Sounds

Trace each letter. Print a List Word that begins with the sound for the letter.

1. _s_ _____

3. _t_ _____

5. _b_ _____

2. _s_ _____

4. _b_ _____

Ending Sounds

Trace each letter. Print a List Word that ends with the sound for the letter.

6. _____ _s_

8. _____ _b_

7. _____ _s_

9. _____ _t_

List Words		
tub	bus	bat
see	sit	us

Missing Words

Print the List Word that completes each sentence.

_____

- - - - - - - - - - - -

1. Here are a ball and a _____.

_____

- - - - - - - - - -

2. I can _____ how I look.

_____

- - - - - - - - - - -

3. Do they see _____?

Spelling Superstar

Writing

What is a good rule for riding on the bus?
Make a sign that tells the rule.

Beginning and Ending h, m, p, k

Get Ready

Read the sentences.

The **map** is on a **hook**.
Sara will show us where she lives.
She will **pin** her name on the map.

Get Set

Read the sentences again. Say each word in dark print. Listen for the beginning and the ending sounds.

 The word **map** begins with the sound for **m.**
It ends with the sound for **p.**

 The word **hook** begins with the sound for **h.**
It ends with the sound for **k.**

 What letter stands for the sound at the beginning of the word **pin**?

29

Go!

Sounds, Letters, and Words

Look at the pictures. Print the letter that stands for the missing beginning sound or ending sound. Trace the letters to spell List Words.

LIST WORDS

1. hot

2. map

3. pin

4. hook

5. hop

6. stop

1. _____ in

2. sto_____

3. _____ ot

4. _____ op

5. hoo_____

6. _____ ap

Beginning Sounds

Name each picture. Print each List Word that begins with the same sound as the picture name.

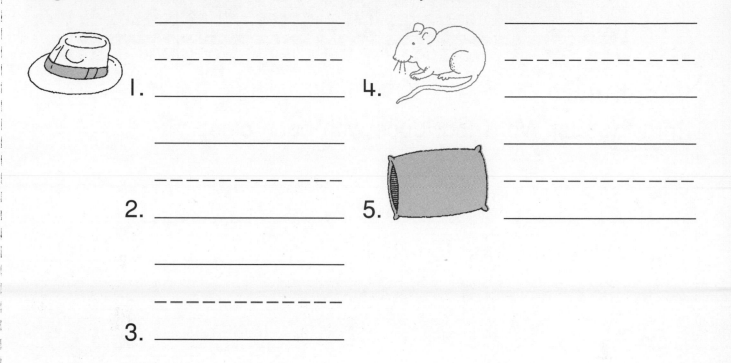

1. _____

2. _____

3. _____

4. _____

5. _____

Ending Sounds

Name each picture. Print each List Word that ends with the same sound as the picture name.

1. _____

2. _____

3. _____

4. _____

List Words

hot	pin	hop
map	hook	stop

Vocabulary

Print the List Word that goes with each clue.

1. It holds something together. _____

2. How does the sun feel? _____

3. Do this before crossing a street. _____

Spelling Superstar

Writing

How can you help a friend
find where you live?
Write a sentence to tell
what you would do.

Beginning and Ending <u>j</u>, <u>f</u>, <u>g</u>

Get Ready

Read the poem.

I have a pet who can
  jump and **jog.**
It isn't a cat, it isn't a dog.
My pet can hop, my pet can dig.
What **fun** it is to have a **pig!**

Get Set

Read the poem again. Say each word in dark print.
Listen for the beginning and the ending sounds.

 The word **jog** begins with the sound for **j.**
It ends with the sound for **g.**

 The word **fun** begins with the sound for **f.**

 What letter stands for the sound at the end
of the word **pig?**

Go!

Sounds, Letters, and Words

Look at the pictures. Print the letter that stands for the missing beginning sound or ending sound. Trace the letters to spell List Words.

LIST WORDS

1. jar
2. fan
3. fun
4. bag
5. jog
6. pig

1. _ _ ba

2. _ _ an

3. _ _ pi

4. _ _ un

5. _ _ ar

6. _ _ jo

Matching

Look at each picture. Then print a List Word
to name each picture.

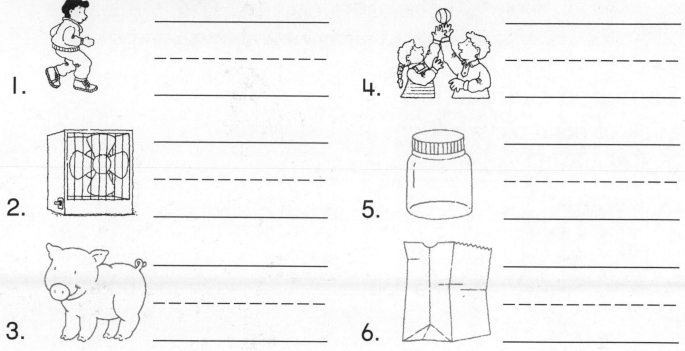

1. _____

2. _____

3. _____

4. _____

5. _____

6. _____

Vocabulary

Print the List Words that end with the same
sound as the picture names.

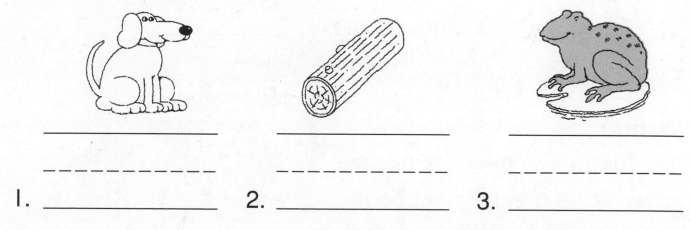

1. _____

2. _____

3. _____

List Words

jar	fun	jog
fan	bag	pig

Sentence Completion

Look at each picture. Print the List Word that completes each sentence.

1. The _____ is in the bag.

2. It is _____ to play.

3. Turn on the _____.

Spelling Superstar

Writing

It is fun to see the pets people have. Write a sentence about one of the pets in the pictures.

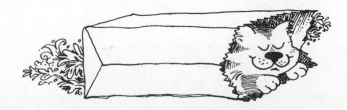

Beginning and Ending l, d, n

Get Ready

Read the sentences.

If you are a **duck,** can you swim
in a pond? If you are a lion, stay in your **den.**
If you are a bird, can you stand on one **leg?**
If you are an ant, go to your **nest.**

Get Set

Read the sentences again. Say each word in dark print.
Listen for the beginning and the ending sounds.

 The word **duck** begins with the sound for **d.**

 The word **den** ends with the sound for **n.** What
sound do you hear at the beginning of **den?**

 The word **leg** begins with the sound for **l.**

 The word **nest** begins with the sound for **n.**

Go!

Sounds, Letters, and Words

Print the letter that stands for the missing beginning sound or ending sound. Trace the letters to spell List Words.

1. _____ og

2. _____ pe

3. _____ eg

4. _____ de

5. _____ uck

6. _____ est

Missing Letters

Print the List Words that fit the shapes.

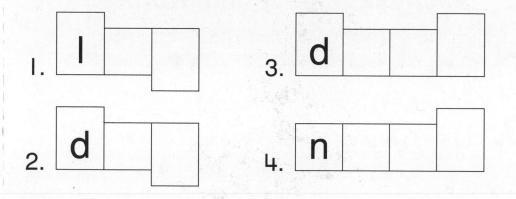

1. l

2. d

3. d

4. n

Vocabulary

Say the name of each picture. Print the List
Word that names each picture.

1. _____

2. _____

3. _____

Rhyming

Print List Words that rhyme with **ten.**

1. _____

2. _____

List Words		
leg	pen	nest
dog	duck	den

Picture Puzzle

Where are they? Print the List Words
that tell where they are.

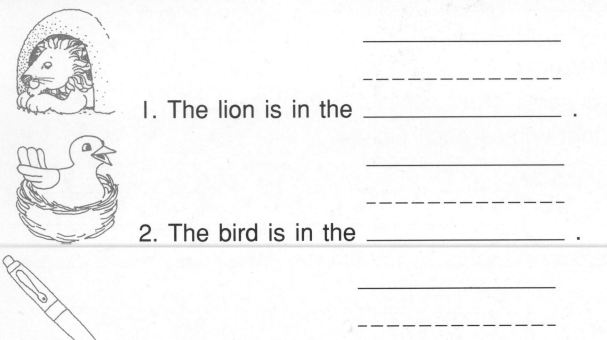

1. The lion is in the _____ .

2. The bird is in the _____ .

3. The ink is in the _____ .

Spelling Superstar

Writing

The duck has a special home.
Write a sentence that tells
about the duck's home.

Beginning and Ending <u>w</u>, <u>c</u>, <u>r</u>

Get Ready

Read the sentences.

Oh! No! It is a **cold, wet** day.
The **car will** not run.
What **can** we do?
We can walk!

Get Set

Read the sentences again. Say each word
in dark print. Listen for the beginning and
the ending sounds.

The word **wet** begins with the sound for **w.**

The word **car** begins with the sound for **c.**
It ends with the sound for **r.** What letter
stands for the sound at the beginning
of the word **can?**

Go!

Sounds, Letters, and Words

Print the letter that stands for the missing beginning sound or ending sound. Trace the letters to spell List Words.

LIST WORDS

1. car
2. can
3. rug
4. wet
5. will
6. cold

1. _____ et
2. _____ ill
3. _____ ug
4. _____ an
5. _____ old
6. _____ ca

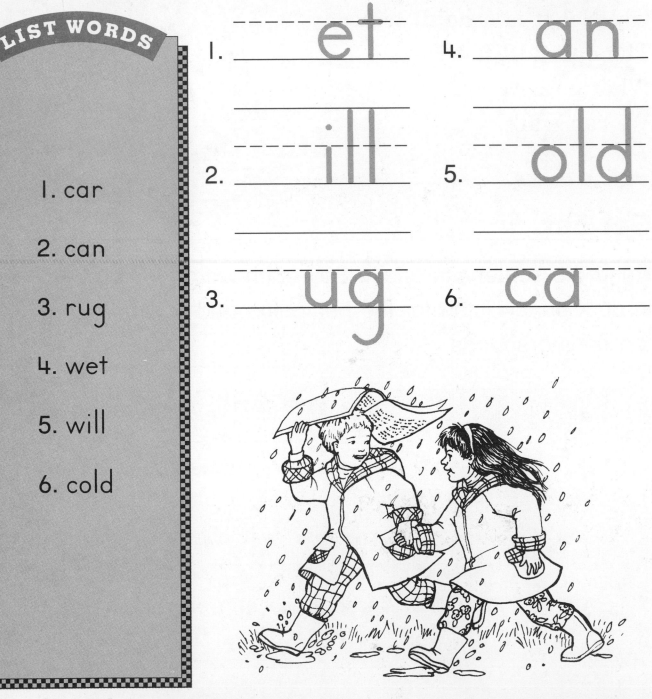

Missing Words

Look at each picture. Then print a
List Word to finish each sentence.

1. The cat sleeps on a _____ .

2. The clothes are still _____ .

3. It is a _____ of corn.

4. She drives her _____ .

5. It is _____ today.

6. I _____ need my coat off.

List Words

car	rug	will
can	wet	cold

Rhyming

Print the List Word that rhymes with each word given.

1. far

_____

- - - - - - - - - - - - - -

_____

2. hill

_____

- - - - - - - - - - - - - -

_____

3. man

_____

- - - - - - - - - - - - - -

4. told

_____

- - - - - - - - - - - - - -

_____

5. met

_____

- - - - - - - - - - - - - -

_____

6. bug

_____

- - - - - - - - - - - - - -

Spelling Superstar

Writing

The weather map tells about the weather. Write a sentence to describe the weather.

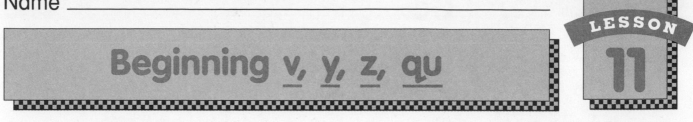

Beginning <u>v</u>, <u>y</u>, <u>z</u>, <u>qu</u>

Get Ready

Read the sentences.

> Can **you** see the **queen** bee? She is **very** big. The other bees **zip** in and out of the hive. They work for the queen bee.

Get Set

Read the sentences again. Say each word in dark print. Listen for the beginning sounds.

 The word **you** begins with the same sound as the word **yo-yo**.

 The word **queen** begins with the sound for **qu**.

 The word **very** begins with the same sound as the word **van**.

 What word begins with the same sound as the word **zoo?**

Go!

Sounds, Letters, and Words

Print the letter or letters that stand for the missing beginning sound. Then trace the letters to spell List Words.

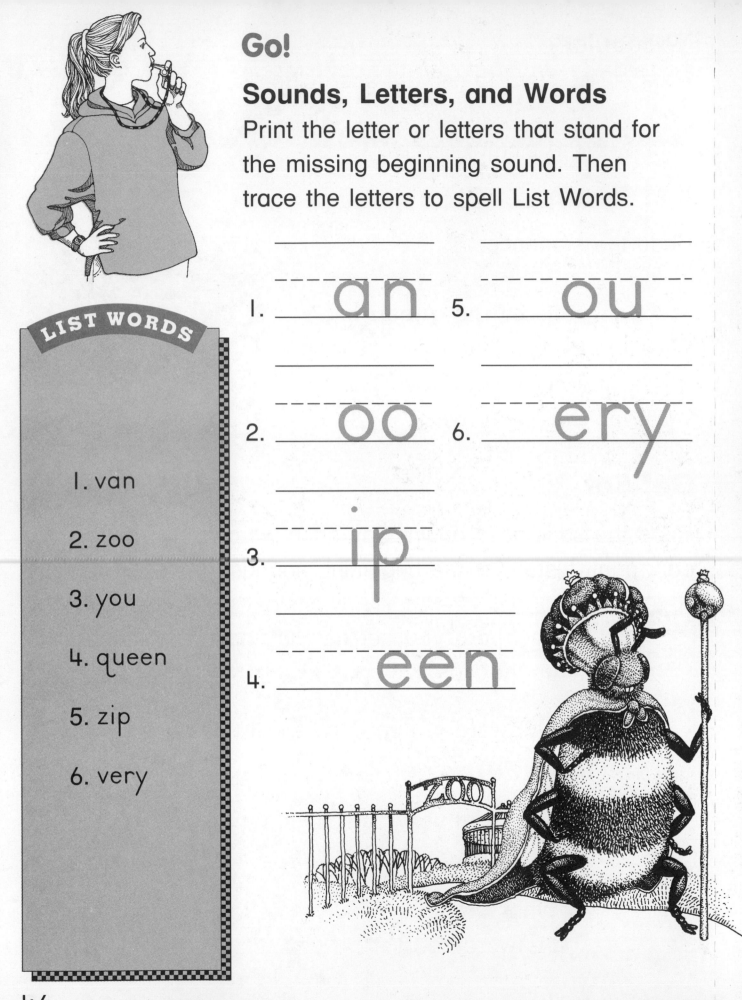

LIST WORDS

1. van

2. zoo

3. you

4. queen

5. zip

6. very

1. ___ an

2. ___ oo

3. ___ ip

4. ___ een

5. ___ ou

6. ___ ery

Vocabulary

Print a List Word to go with each clue.
The List Word begins with the same
sound as the picture name.

1. Animals live here.

_____

2. She lives with the king.

_____

3. You can ride in this.

_____

Rhyming

Print a List Word that rhymes with each
picture. The word shapes will help you.

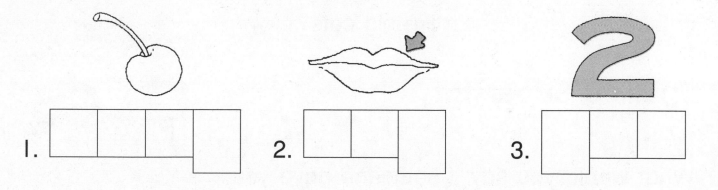

1. ⬜⬜⬜⬜

2. ⬜⬜⬜

3. ⬜⬜⬜

List Words

van	you	zip
zoo	queen	very

Missing Words

Look at the picture. Then print
List Words to finish the story.
The word shapes will help you.

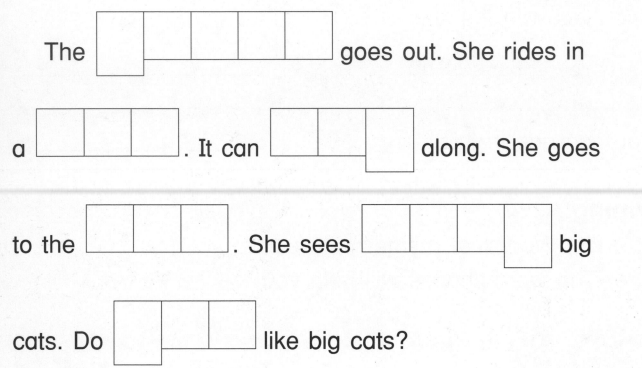

The ⬚⬚⬚⬚⬚ goes out. She rides in

a ⬚⬚⬚. It can ⬚⬚⬚⬚ along. She goes

to the ⬚⬚⬚. She sees ⬚⬚⬚⬚ big

cats. Do ⬚⬚⬚ like big cats?

Spelling Superstar

Writing

What would you say if someone gave you
a big jar of honey? Write a thank-you
note that tells what you would say.

Ending <u>x</u>, <u>k</u>, <u>p</u>

Get Ready

Read the sentences.

This **book** tells you how to make a good trail snack! You will need:

- **six** large spoons of cereal
- one small **box** of raisins
- three spoons of nuts

Mix in a big bowl. **Pop** some in your mouth!

Get Set

Read the sentences again. Say each word in dark print. Listen for the ending sounds.

The word **book** ends with the sound for **k**.

The word **six** ends with the sound for **x**.

What sound do you hear at the end of the word **pop?**

49

Go!

Sounds, Letters, and Words

Print the letter that stands for the missing ending sound. Trace the letters to spell List Words.

LIST WORDS

1. six
2. box
3. top
4. book
5. mix
6. pop

1. po
2. mi
3. boo

4. si
5. to
6. bo

Rhyming

Read each set of words. Print the two words in each set that rhyme.

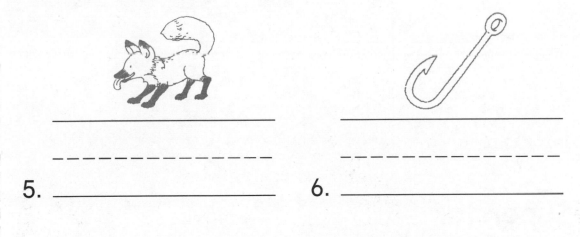

six   book   mix

_____   _____

- - - - - - - - - -   - - - - - - - - - -

1. _____   2. _____

box   pop   top

_____   _____

- - - - - - - - - -   - - - - - - - - - -

3. _____   4. _____

Say the name of each picture. Print the List Word that rhymes with it.

_____   _____

- - - - - - - - - -   - - - - - - - - - -

5. _____   6. _____

Puzzle

Print a List Word in the puzzle
to name each picture.

ACROSS

DOWN

2.

5.

6.

1.

3.

4.

Spelling Superstar

Writing

The sandwich looks good.
Write about how you make
your favorite sandwich.

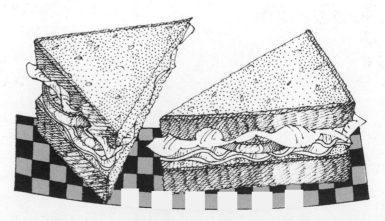

Instant Replay • Lessons 6–12

Time Out

You have learned the sounds that the consonants spell when they come at the beginning or the end of words. Now it's time to review what you have learned.

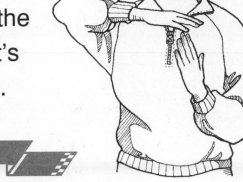

Lesson 6

The letters **s, t,** and **b** stand for the sounds at the beginning or the end of some words.

List Words
bat
bus
tub
sit

Print the List Word that names each picture.

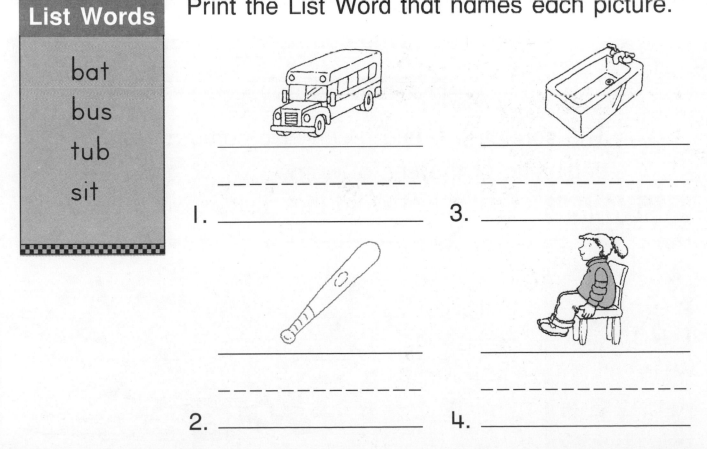

1. _____

2. _____

3. _____

4. _____

Other words begin or end with the sounds **h, m, p,** and **k.**

List Words

hop

hook

map

pin

Look at each picture. Print a List Word to complete each sentence.

1. That _____ can't catch me!

2. The _____ will help me.

3. I can use this big _____ .

4. Who can _____ the fastest?

The sounds **j, f,** and **g** can also come at the beginning or the end of words.

Print a List Word that rhymes with each word.

List Words

fun

jar

jog

pig

1. dig _____

2. car _____

3. sun _____

4. hog _____

Some words begin or end with the sounds **l, d,** and **n.** Name each picture. Print a List Word that begins with the same sound.

List Words

dog

pen

leg

nest

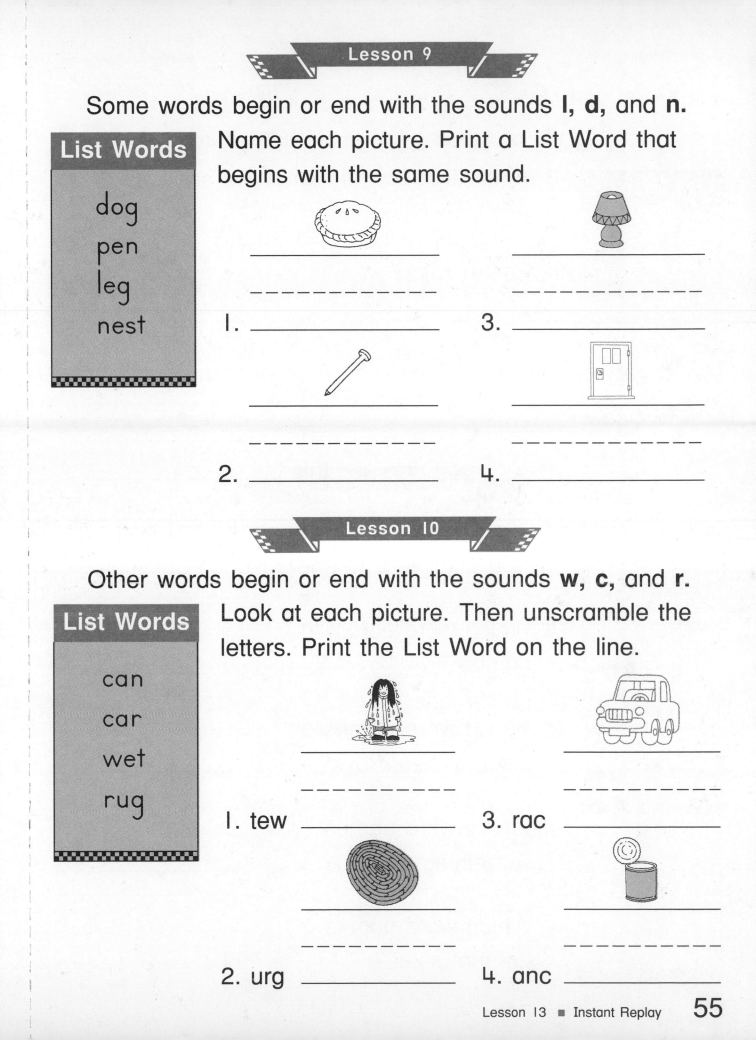

1. _____

2. _____

3. _____

4. _____

Other words begin or end with the sounds **w, c,** and **r.** Look at each picture. Then unscramble the letters. Print the List Word on the line.

List Words

can

car

wet

rug

1. tew _____

2. urg _____

3. rac _____

4. anc _____

The letters **v, y, z,** and **qu** stand for the sounds at the beginning of some words.

Print the List Words that fit the shapes.

List Words

queen

van

you

zip

1.

2.

3.

4.

Other words end with the sounds **x, k,** and **p.**

Print a List Word to answer each question.

List Words

book

box

six

top

1. Which word names a number?

2. Which word names a place to keep toys?

3. Which word names something to read?

4. Which word names a toy that spins?

Short a Sound

Get Ready

Read the poem.

Who is the lady?
What does she see?
Why is a **lamp** in her **hand?**
She is the one who stands for liberty.
Her light shines over our land.
From the green of the hills,
To the blue of the sea,
Her light is for you **and** for me.

Get Set

Read the poem again. Say each word in
dark print. Listen for the short **a** sounds.

You can hear the short **a** sound in **hand.**
What sound do you hear in the words
lamp and **and?**

Go!

Sounds, Letters, and Words

Print the missing letters in each word.
Trace the letters to spell List Words.

LIST WORDS

1. hat
2. man
3. has
4. lamp
5. and
6. hand

1. m _____
2. h _____
3. h _____
4. a _____
5. h _____
6. l _____

Missing Words

Look at each picture. Then print a List Word
to finish each sentence.

1. Turn on the _____.

2. Vicki _____ Nancy are sisters.

3. Burt _____ a new book.

4. Sharon is wearing a pretty _____.

Word Groups

Print the List Word that belongs with each
group of words.

1. foot, arm, _____

2. bed, table, _____

3. boy, girl, _____

4. dress, shoe, _____

List Words		
hat	has	and
man	lamp	hand

Vocabulary

Print the List Word that goes with each clue.

1. owns or holds _____

2. part of the body _____

3. a grown-up boy _____

4. also or added to _____

Spelling Superstar

Writing

Many statues show great people. Do you know who this statue shows? Write about this statue or another statue you know.

Short i Sound

Get Ready

Read the sentences.

Did you ever **hit** the ball and **win** the game? **This** girl **did.** It was the **big** game. The score was tied. The bases were loaded. She stepped up to the plate. She swung the bat and hit the ball. It was a home run!

Get Set

Read the sentences again.
Say each word in dark print.
Listen for the short **i** sound.

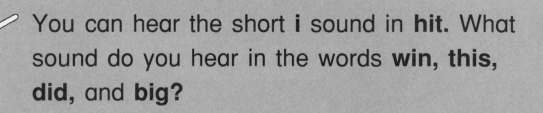

You can hear the short **i** sound in **hit.** What sound do you hear in the words **win, this, did,** and **big?**

Go!

Sounds, Letters, and Words

Print an **i** in each word. Trace the letters to spell List Words.

LIST WORDS

1. hit
2. big
3. win
4. fill
5. this
6. did

1. b_g

2. d_d

3. th_s

4. f_ll

5. h_t

6. w_n

Missing Words

Print a List Word to answer each question.
The word shapes will help you.

1. Will you do your homework? I ⬚⬚ it.

2. Why are you in the race? I want to ⬚⬚ .

3. What do you do with the bat? I ⬚⬚ the ball.

4. Do you want some milk? Yes, you can ⬚⬚ my glass.

ABC Order

Print each pair of List Words in ABC order.

big   fill

_____   _____

1. _____   _____

win   this

_____   _____

2. _____   _____

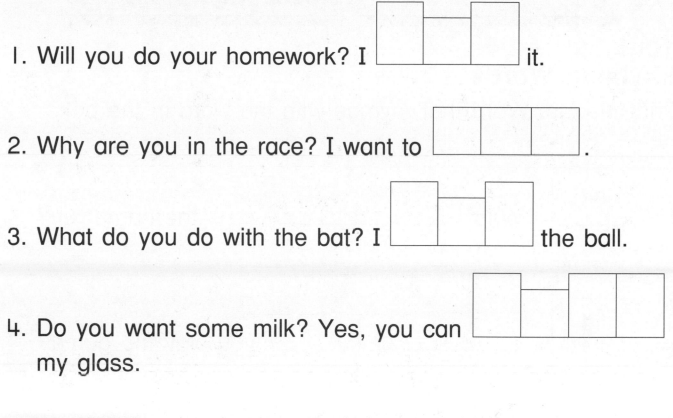

List Words

hit	win	this
big	fill	did

Rhyming Words

Print the List Word that rhymes with the word in the box.

1. | sit |

Who _____ the home run?

2. | lid |

_____ you play the game?

3. | miss |

Please wash _____ cup.

4. | pig |

What a _____ dog!

Spelling Superstar

Writing

Do you have a favorite game? What is it called? Write some sentences that tell how to play the game.

Short u̲ Sound

Get Ready

Read the poem.

If I were a kangaroo
I know **just** what I'd do.
I'd bounce around the house a lot
And in the backyard too.
I'd **run** and **jump**
And play all day.
And when the day was through,
I'd wash my face
And paws because
I am a kangaroo.

Get Set

Read the poem again. Say each word in dark
print. Listen for the short **u** sound.

Listen for the short **u** sound in **jump.**
What sound do you hear in the words **just**
and **run?**

Go!

Sounds, Letters, and Words

Print letters to finish each word.
Trace the letters to spell List Words.
The word shapes will help you.

1. s
2. j   p
3. j   t

4. h
5. r
6. b

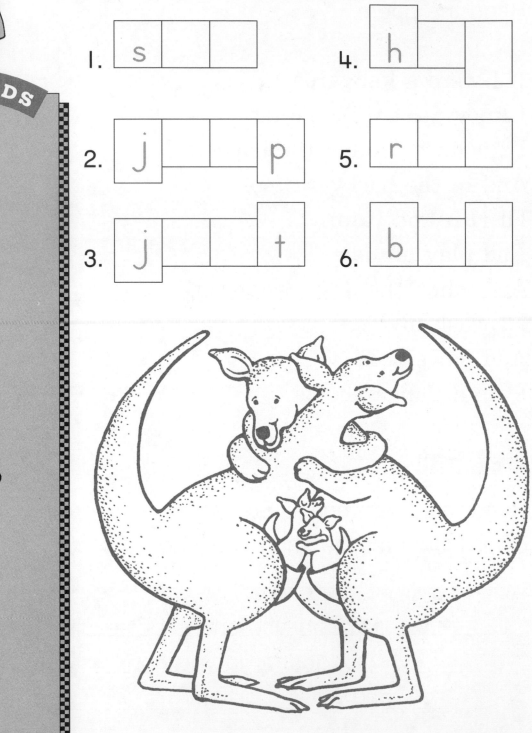

66   Lesson 16 ■ Short **u** Sound

Rhyming

Print the List Word that rhymes with each word.

_____   _____

1. bug _____   2. pump _____

ABC Order

Print each pair of List Words in ABC order.

but hug

_____   _____

1. _____   _____

sun jump

_____   _____

2. _____   _____

just run

_____   _____

3. _____   _____

Puzzle

Use List Words to solve the puzzle. Print the letters in the boxes.

ACROSS

2. Kangaroos do this a lot.
3. It shines on the earth.
4. It rhymes with **cut.**

DOWN

1. It means to move in a big hurry.
2. It rhymes with **must.**

Spelling Superstar

Writing

What would you do if a kangaroo visited you? Write about how you might show it a good time.

Short o Sound

Get Ready

Read the sentences.

It's a **lot** of fun to grow a plant. First, get a carrot. Cut **off** the end. Put it in a small dish. Pour in water to cover the bottom of the dish. **Not** too much! Place the dish in sunlight. Water your plant when the dish is dry.

Get Set

Read the sentences again. Say each word in dark print. Listen for the short **o** sound.

You can hear the short **o** sound in **off.** What sound do you hear in the words **lot** and **not?**

Go!

Sounds, Letters, and Words

Print the missing letters for each word.
Trace the letters to spell List Words.

1. d _ _ _

2. o _ _ _

3. l _ _ _

4. n _ _ _

5. g _ _ _

6. j _ _ _

LIST WORDS

1. lot
2. got
3. not
4. job
5. drop
6. off

Missing Words

Look at each picture. Then print a List Word
to finish each sentence.

1. "This is a hard _____."

2. "I hope I don't _____ it."

3. "Do _____ be sad, Bear."

4. "I have a _____ of friends, Bear."

5. "I've _____ friends to help me."

6. "My friends flew _____ with my box."

Scrambled Letters

Unscramble the letters to spell List Words.
Print the words on the lines.

1. ffo _____

2. ton _____

3. jbo _____

4. otl _____

5. tog _____

6. ropd _____

Spelling Superstar

Writing

Plants need care. Write about how
you would take care of a plant.

Short e Sound

Get Ready

Read the riddle.

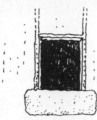

One hen is in the barnyard.
Two hens **rest** on a stoop.
Three hens **went** off to wander.
Ten hens are in the coop.
If you add them up
    before the sun comes up,
    how many hens will crow?

None. Only roosters crow.

Get Set

Read the riddle again. Say each word in
dark print. Listen for the short **e** sound.

10 You can hear the short **e** sound in **ten.** What
vowel sound do you hear in the words **rest**
and **went?**

Go!

Sounds, Letters, and Words

Print an **e** in each word. Trace the letters to spell List Words.

1. ___ n d

2. w ___ n t

3. r ___ s t

4. j ___ t

5. r ___ d

6. t ___ n

LIST WORDS

1. ten

2. red

3. jet

4. went

5. end

6. rest

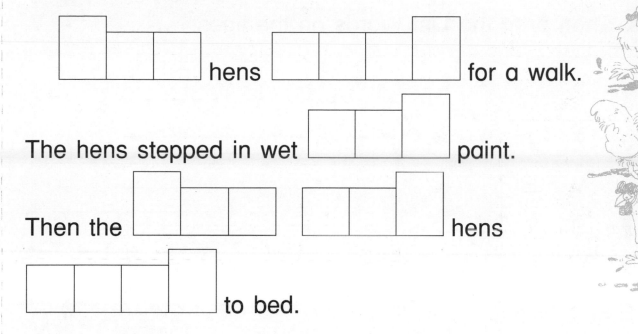

Missing Words

Print List Words to finish the silly story. You may use a word more than once. The word shapes will help you.

☐☐☐ hens ☐☐☐ for a walk.

The hens stepped in wet ☐☐☐ paint.

Then the ☐☐☐ ☐☐☐ hens

☐☐☐☐ to bed.

Word Clues

Print the List Word that goes with each clue.

1. This is a fast plane.

_____

_____

3. This comes last.

_____

_____

2. You have this many toes.

_____

_____

4. Do this if you are tired.

_____

_____

List Words

ten	jet	end
red	went	rest

Puzzle

Circle the List Words in the puzzle. The words go across. Then print the List Words on the lines.

```
C  J  E  T
M  Z  V  E
R  E  S  T
T  X  H  R
I  E  N  D
```

1. _____

2. _____

3. _____

Spelling Superstar

Writing

Read the sentences. Write more sentences about the ten red hens.

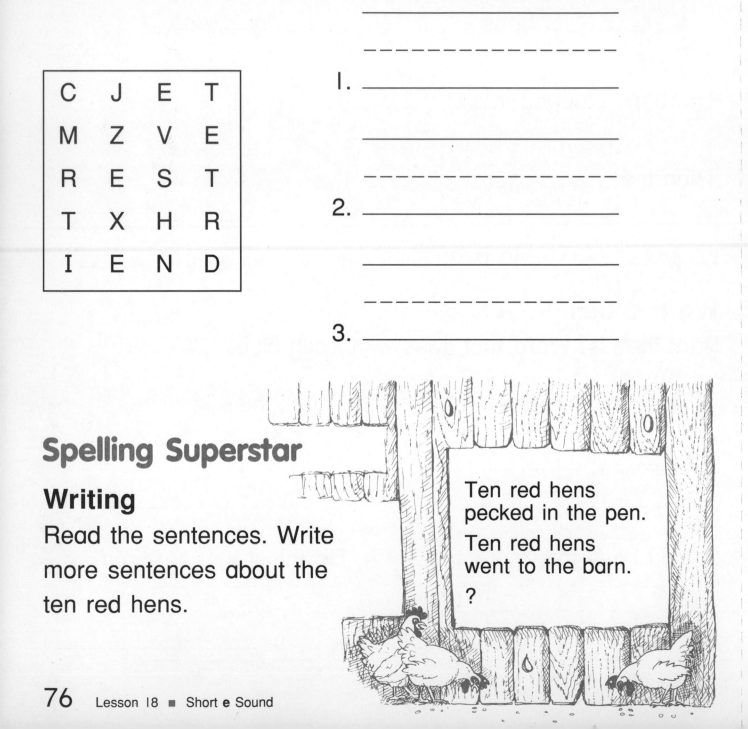

Ten red hens pecked in the pen.

Ten red hens went to the barn.

?

Instant Replay • Lessons 14–18

Time Out

Now it's time to review what you have learned about words that have short vowel sounds.

Lesson 14

The vowels have long and short sounds.
Listen for the short **a** sound in <u>has</u>.

List Words
hand
lamp
man
hat

Print the List Word that names each picture.

1. _____

3. _____

2. _____

4. _____

You can hear the short **i** sound in <u>win</u> and <u>fill</u>. Print a List Word that rhymes with each word given.

List Words

big
did
hit
this

1. fit _____   3. kiss _____

2. hid _____   4. dig _____

Listen for the short **u** sound in <u>but</u> and <u>just</u>. Look at each picture. Print the List Word that completes each sentence.

List Words

hug
jump
run
sun

1. Give me a big _____.

2. The _____ is hot.

3. I can't _____ fast.

4. I can _____ high!

You can hear the short **o** sound in <u>lot</u> and <u>not</u>.
Print these List Words in ABC order.

List Words

drop

off

job

got

1. _____

2. _____

3. _____

4. _____

Listen for the short **e** sound in <u>red</u> and <u>went</u>.
Look at each picture. Then unscramble the
letters. Print each List Word correctly.

List Words

end

jet

rest

ten

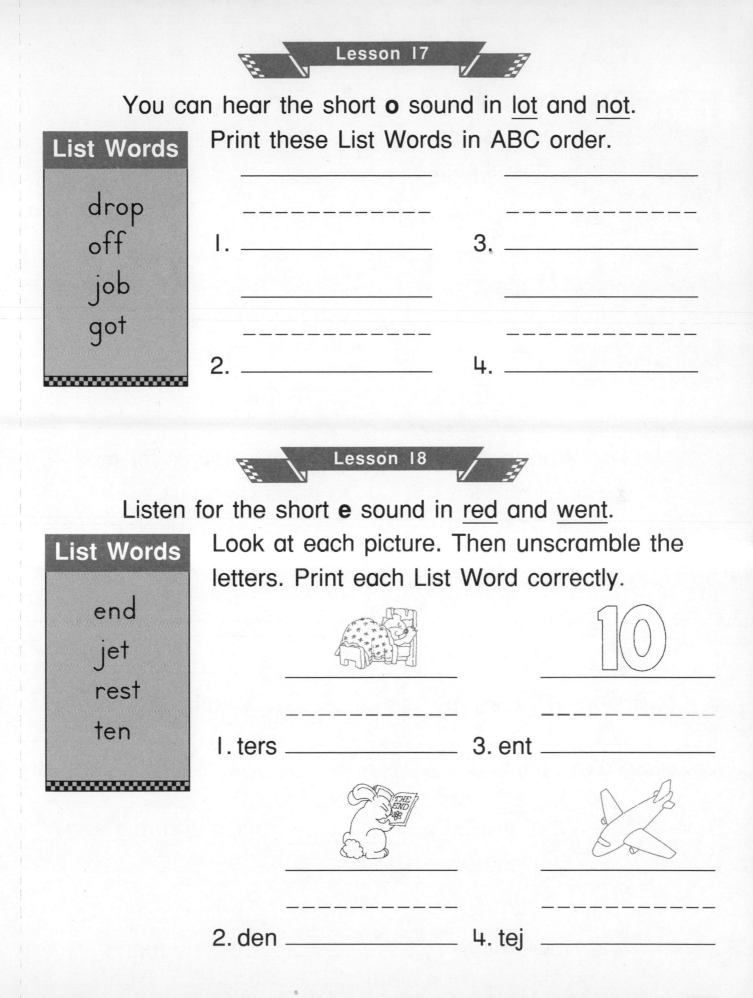

1. ters _____

2. den _____

3. ent _____

4. tej _____

List Words

jump

hat

rest

big

job

got

Look at each picture. Then complete each sentence. Print the List Word that makes sense.

1. One egg is small,

_____

_ _ _ _ _ _ _ _ _ _ _

and one is _____.

2. _____

_ _ _ _ _ _ _ _ _ _ _

What a hard _____ this is for me!

3. _____

_ _ _ _ _ _ _ _ _ _ _

I need to sit and _____.

4. _____

_ _ _ _ _ _ _ _ _ _ _

I will take my _____ off.

5. _____

_ _ _ _ _ _ _ _ _ _ _

What will _____ out of that big egg?

6. _____

_ _ _ _ _ _ _ _ _ _ _

Now I have _____ a new friend!

LESSON

20

Long a Sound

Get Ready

Read the sentences.

Her **name** is Bitsy. She is a baby elephant. Bitsy lives with a circus. When she is happy, she will **make** a noise with her trunk. It sounds like a trumpet! Bitsy played a **game** with the children who **came** to see her. She tickled them with her trunk. This made Bitsy happy and she made her trumpet sound!

Get Set

Read the sentences again. Say each word in dark print. Listen for the long **a** sound.

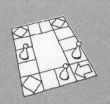

You can hear the long **a** sound in **game.** What sound do you hear in the words **name, make,** and **came?**

Go!

Sounds, Letters, and Words

Print the missing letters in the words.
Trace the letters to spell List Words.

LIST WORDS

1. make
2. came
3. gave
4. name
5. take
6. game
7. place
8. bake

1. g v
2. c m
3. p l c
4. t k

5. b k
6. n m
7. g m
8. m k

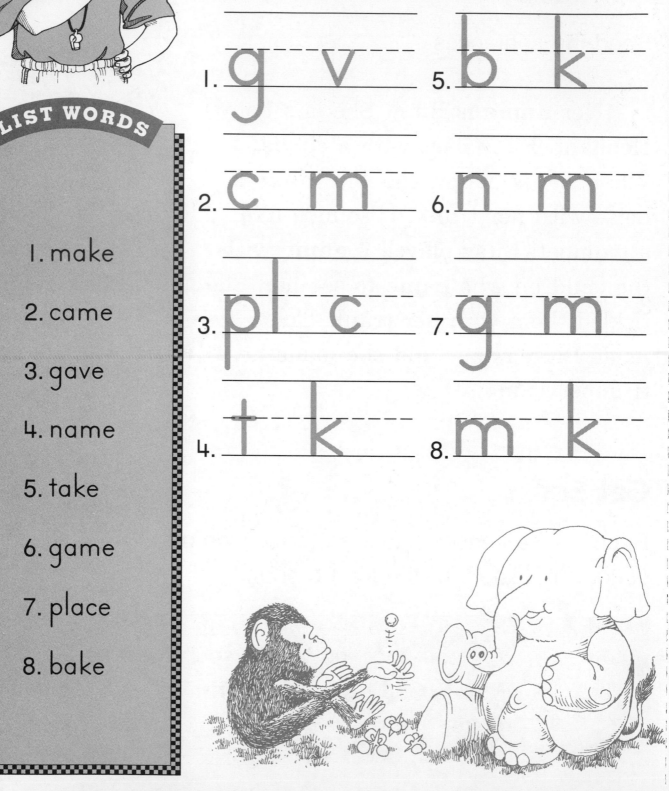

Puzzle

Circle each List Word in the puzzle. The word can go across or up and down. Then print the List Words on the lines.

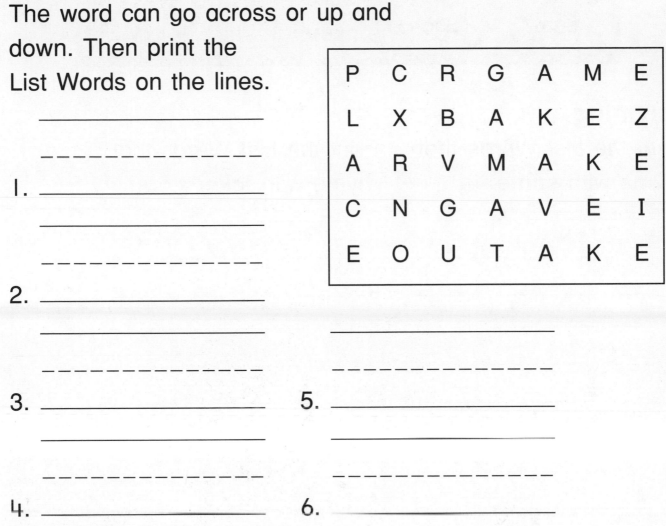

```
P  C  R  G  A  M  E
L  X  B  A  K  E  Z
A  R  V  M  A  K  E
C  N  G  A  V  E  I
E  O  U  T  A  K  E
```

1. _____

2. _____

3. _____

4. _____

5. _____

6. _____

ABC Order

Print these List Words in ABC order: **name, came, gave, place.** The word shapes will help you.

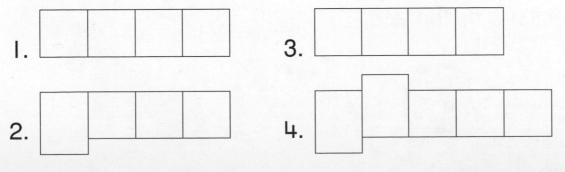

1.

2.

3.

4.

Rhyming

Print the List Words that rhyme with **same.**

Print the List Words that rhyme with **lake.**

1. _____

2. _____

3. _____

4. _____

5. _____

6. _____

Spelling Superstar

Writing

Do you like elephants? Tell about an elephant you have seen at the circus or the zoo.

LESSON
21

Long i Sound

Get Ready

Read the poem.

I **like** to read.
I like to write.
I like to fly a **kite.**
I like to swim.
I like to hike.
I like to **ride** my **bike.**
When I am sad,
To make me glad,
I think of things I like.

Get Set

Read the poem again. Say each word in
dark print. Listen for the long **i** sound.

You can hear the long **i** sound in **kite.**
What sound do you hear in the words **like,**
ride, and **bike?**

Go!

Sounds, Letters, and Words

Print the missing **i** and **e** in each word.
Trace the letters to spell List Words.

1. l __ k __

2. r __ d __

3. f __ v __

4. m __ n __

5. d __ m __

6. k __ t __

7. b __ k __

8. t __ m __

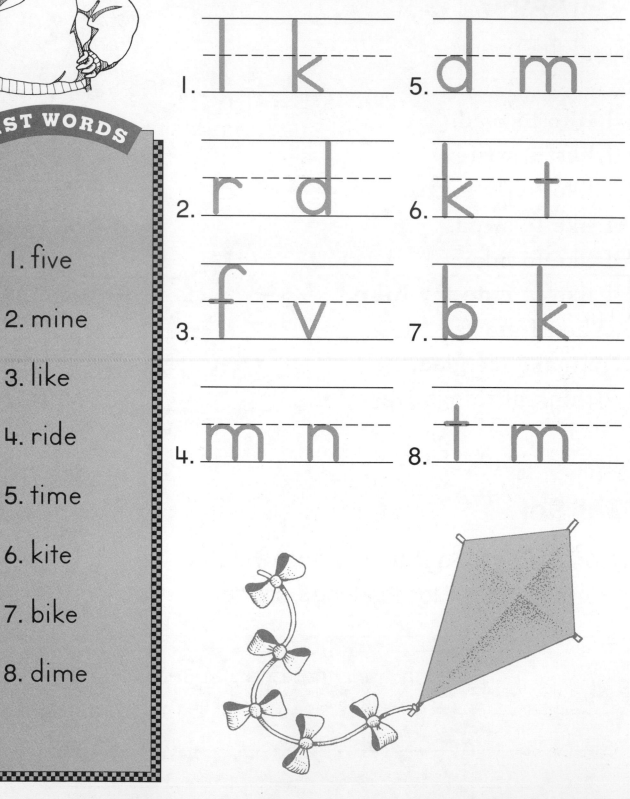

Missing Words

Print List Words to finish the story.
The word shapes will help you.

Today I will ☐☐☐ to town. I will go on a ☐☐. It is ☐☐☐☐. Do you

☐☐ it? I will take a ☐☐☐

to buy lemonade. At ☐☐☐ I will come home. Then

it will be ☐☐☐☐ for dinner.

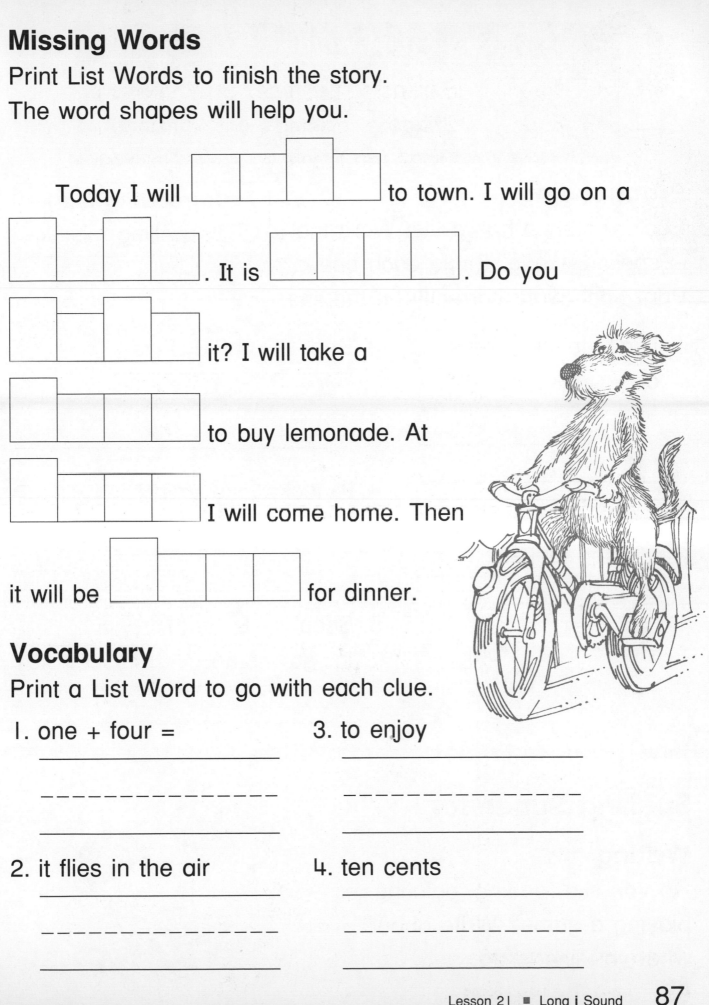

Vocabulary

Print a List Word to go with each clue.

1. one + four =

_____

_____

2. it flies in the air

_____

_____

3. to enjoy

_____

_____

4. ten cents

_____

_____

List Words

five	like	time	bike
mine	ride	kite	dime

Proofreading

Each sentence has a List Word that is spelled wrong. Circle each one. Print each word correctly on the line.

Proofreading Marks

⬭ spelling mistake

1. I go to the park on a bik.

   _____

   _ _ _ _ _ _ _ _ _ _ _ _ _ _

   _____

2. I riad the ponies there.

   _____

   _ _ _ _ _ _ _ _ _ _ _ _ _ _

   _____

3. See the blue kyte.

   _____

   _ _ _ _ _ _ _ _ _ _ _ _ _ _

   _____

4. It looks like min.

   _____

   _ _ _ _ _ _ _ _ _ _ _ _ _ _

   _____

5. Soon it is tiem to go home.

   _____

   _ _ _ _ _ _ _ _ _ _ _ _ _ _

   _____

Spelling Superstar

Writing

Do you like reading, painting, or playing a game? Write about what you like to do.

Long o Sound

Get Ready

Read the sentences.

A bear will spend the winter in a cave. Most birds will fly south. Where will a **toad** live when it gets cold? Where will his winter **home** be?

In the fall, he will dig a hole in the mud. He will climb in. Then he will **fold** leaves over to cover himself. What will he do next? He will sleep until the spring!

Get Set

Read the sentences again. Say each word in dark print. Listen for the long **o** sound.

 You can hear the long **o** sound in **toad.** What sound do you hear in the words **home** and **fold?**

Go!

Sounds, Letters, and Words

Print each List Word under the way the long **o** sound is spelled.

__oa__

1. _____

2. _____

3. _____

__oe

4. _____

__o__e

5. _____

6. _____

__o__ __

7. _____

8. _____

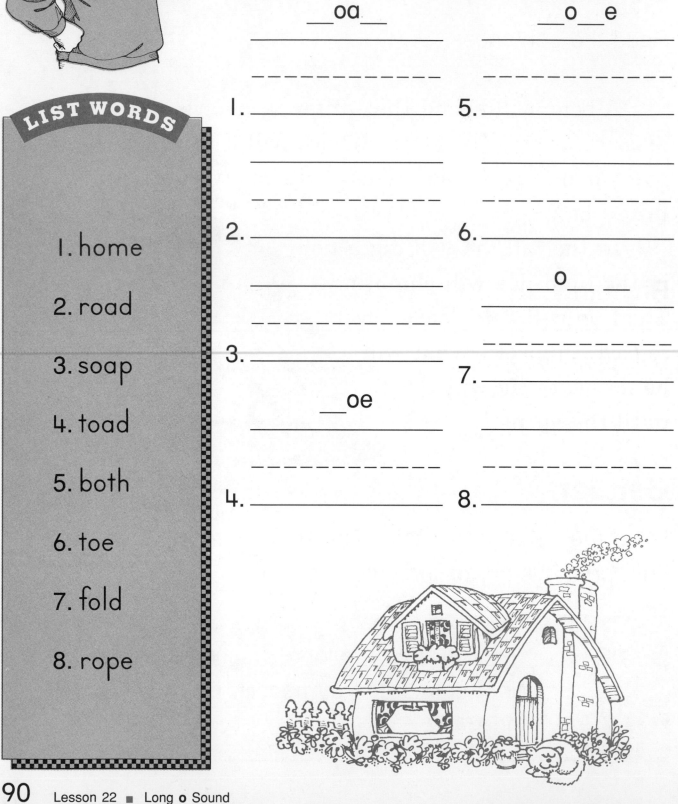

Scrambled Letters

Unscramble the letters to spell List Words. The word shapes will help you to print the words.

1. odat

4. apos

2. ote

5. dolf

3. thob

6. omeh

Rhyming

Print each List Word that rhymes with the word given.

1. doe

2. cold

3. load

4. hope

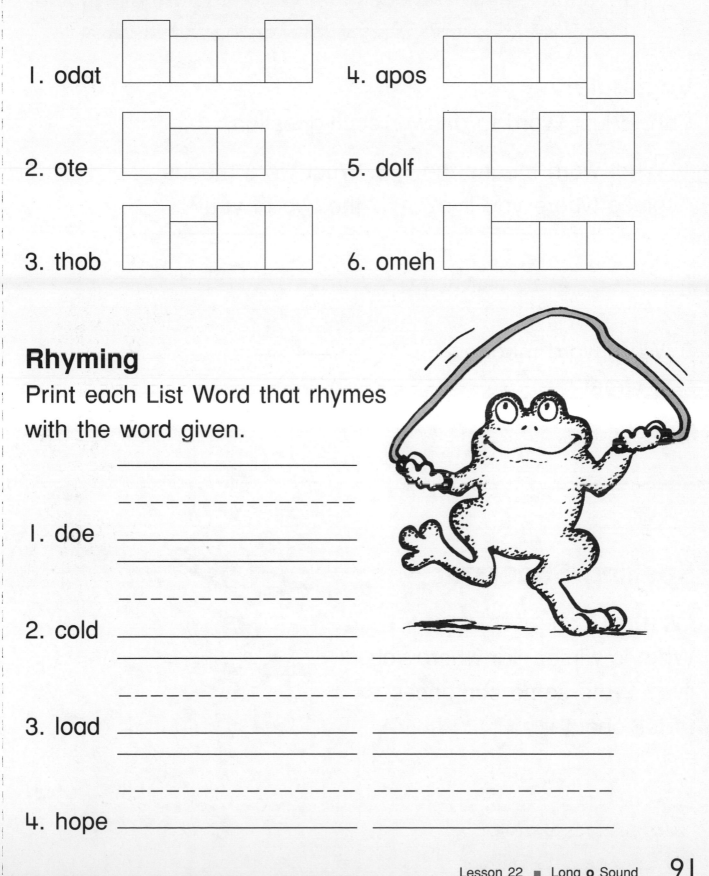

List Words

home	soap	both	fold
road	toad	toe	rope

Vocabulary

Print a List Word to answer each question.

1. What word means the place where you live?

_____

- - - - - - - - - - - - - -

_____

3. What word means the two of you?

_____

- - - - - - - - - - - - - -

_____

2. What word means a street?

_____

- - - - - - - - - - - - - -

_____

Spelling Superstar

Writing

What is winter like where you live? Write some sentences to tell about it.

Long e Sound

Get Ready

Read the sentences.

Would you like to see more birds in your yard? If so, feed them! Birds will **eat** lots of foods. Seeds or crumbs make a great bird **meal.** Birds also like apples. Hang an apple from the branch of a **tree.** Try to count how many new birds come to visit!

Get Set

Read the sentences again. Say each word in dark print. Listen for the long **e** sound.

You can hear the long **e** sound in **tree.** What sound do you hear in the words **eat** and **meal?**

Go!

Sounds, Letters, and Words

Print each List Word under the way the long **e** sound is spelled.

e

_____
_ _ _ _ _ _ _ _ _ _ _ _
1. _____

ee

_____
_ _ _ _ _ _ _ _ _ _ _ _
2. _____

_____
_ _ _ _ _ _ _ _ _ _ _ _
3. _____

_____
_ _ _ _ _ _ _ _ _ _ _ _
4. _____

ea

_____
_ _ _ _ _ _ _ _ _ _ _ _
5. _____

_____
_ _ _ _ _ _ _ _ _ _ _ _
6. _____

_____
_ _ _ _ _ _ _ _ _ _ _ _
7. _____

_____
_ _ _ _ _ _ _ _ _ _ _ _
8. _____

LIST WORDS

1. we
2. eat
3. meal
4. tree
5. three
6. feet
7. heat
8. neat

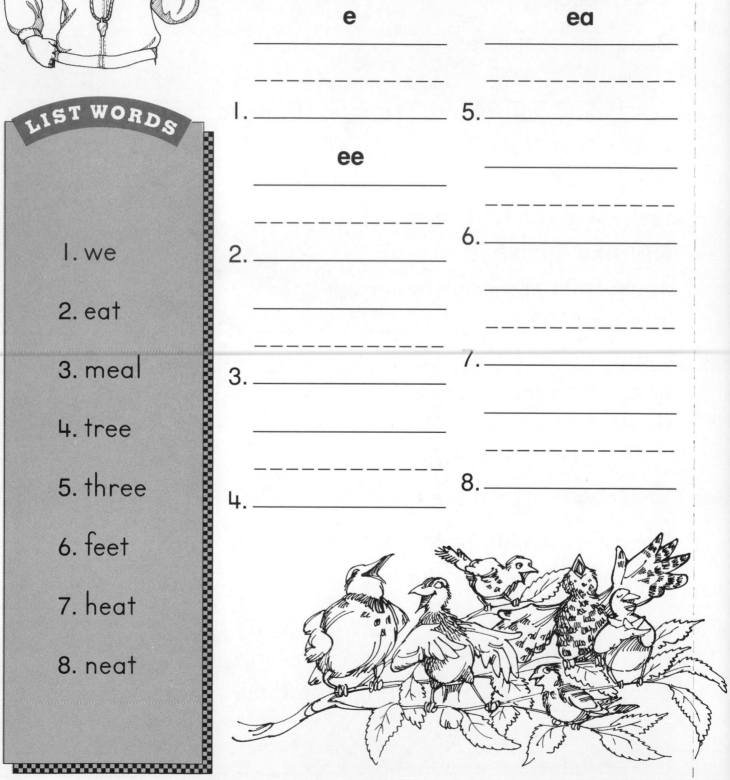

ABC Order

Print each set of List Words in ABC order.

meal   feet   heat

1. _____ _____ _____

eat   three   neat

2. _____ _____ _____

Riddles

Print a List Word to answer each riddle.
The word shapes will help you.

1. You and I are this.

2. Breakfast is one.

3. You walk with these.

4. Birds sit in it.

5. You feel it when you sit next to a fire.

6. Two apples and one more

List Words

we	meal	three	heat
eat	tree	feet	neat

Proofreading

Read the story. Four List Words are spelled wrong. Circle each one. Then print each word correctly on the line.

Proofreading Marks

◯ spelling mistake

My sister and I have a playhouse in a tre. Wie play games there. We like to ete our lunch there. We keep our playhouse clean and neet.

1. _____

2. _____

3. _____

4. _____

Spelling Superstar

Writing

Look at the birds in the tree.
Write a poem about them.
Use List Words in your poem.

ou Sound

Get Ready

Read the sentences.

Do you have things you'd like to save? Make a scrapbook. Here's **how.** Look **around** your **house** for pieces of poster board or heavy paper. Cut the pieces into the page size you like. Punch **out** holes at the sides. Tie the pieces together with old shoelaces or string. Then paste the things you want to save on the pages.

Get Set

Read the sentences again. Say each word in dark print. Listen for the **ou** sound.

You can hear the **ou** sound in **house.** What sound do you hear in the words **how, around,** and **out?**

Go!

Sounds, Letters, and Words

Print each List Word under the way the **ou** sound is spelled.

1. _____   7. _____

2. _____   8. _____

3. _____

4. _____

5. _____

6. _____

1. out

2. our

3. down

4. how

5. found

6. house

7. mouse

8. around

Story Puzzle

Print List Words to finish the story.

_____

- - - - - - - - - - - - - -

I have a pet _____. One day it got

_____   _____

- - - - - - - -   - - - - - - - - - - - - -

_____ of the cage. It ran all _____

_____   _____

- - - - - - - - - - -   - - - - - - - - -

the _____. _____ can I find it?

Puzzle

Circle each List Word in the puzzle.
Print the List Words on the lines.

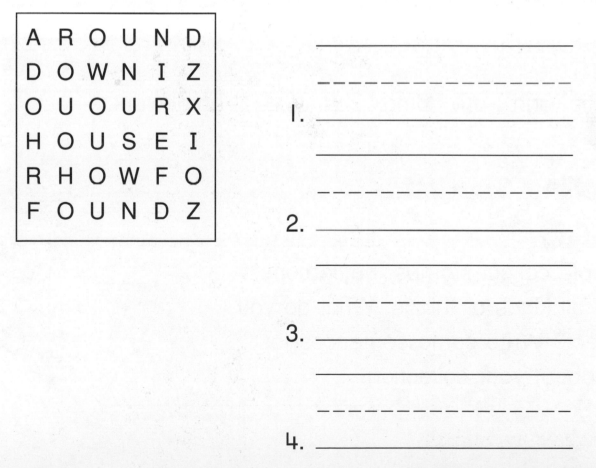

```
A R O U N D
D O W N I Z
O U O U R X
H O U S E I
R H O W F O
F O U N D Z
```

1. _____

   - - - - - - - - - - - - - - -

2. _____

   - - - - - - - - - - - - - - -

3. _____

   - - - - - - - - - - - - - - -

4. _____

Missing Words

Print a List Word to complete each sentence.
The word shapes will help you.

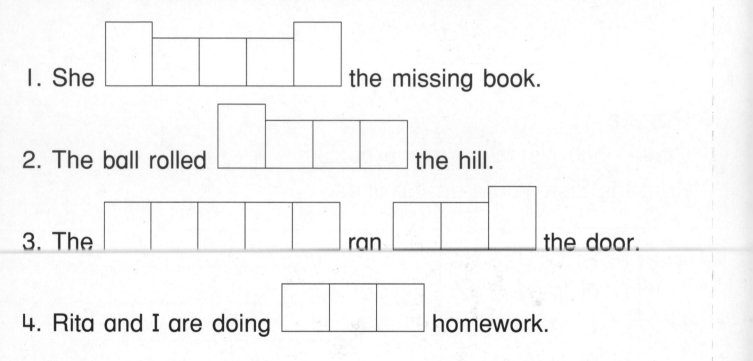

1. She _____ the missing book.

2. The ball rolled _____ the hill.

3. The _____ ran _____ the door.

4. Rita and I are doing _____ homework.

Spelling Superstar

Writing

People collect stamps, bottle caps, and all kinds of things. What do you collect? Write some sentences to tell about your collection.

Instant Replay • Lessons 20–24

Time Out

Take another look at words with long vowel sounds and the **ou** sound.

Lesson 20

Sometimes **a** and **e** together in a word make the long **a** sound, as in <u>game</u>.

List Words

make

came

bake

name

Print the List Words that rhyme with each picture's name.

1. _____

2. _____

3. _____

4. _____

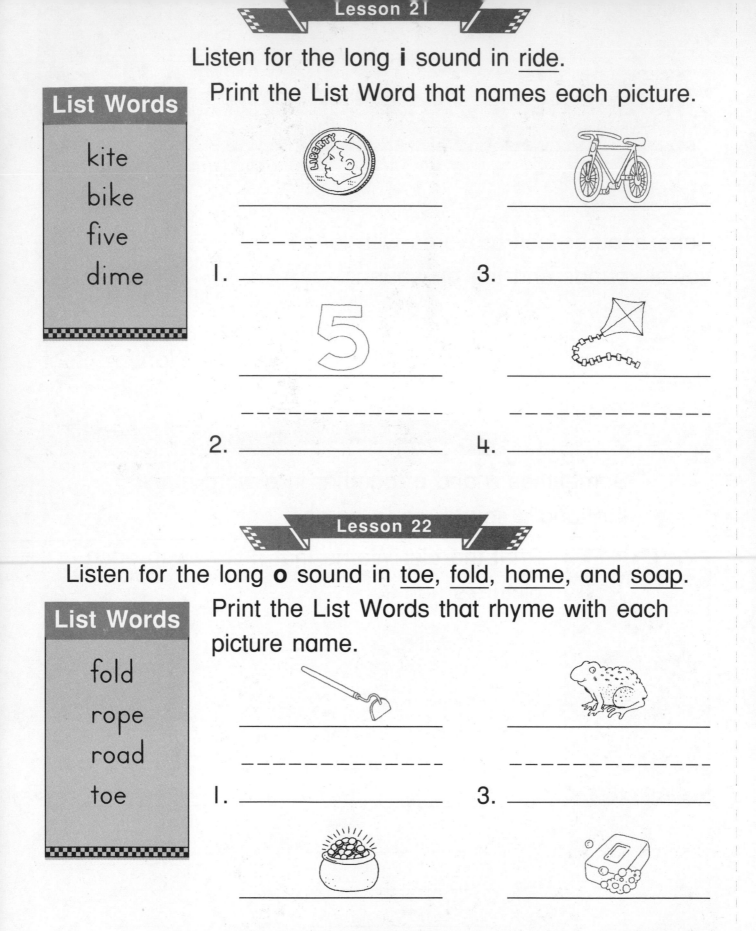

Listen for the long **i** sound in <u>ride</u>.

Print the List Word that names each picture.

List Words

kite

bike

five

dime

1. _____

2. _____

3. _____

4. _____

Listen for the long **o** sound in <u>toe</u>, <u>fold</u>, <u>home</u>, and <u>soap</u>.

Print the List Words that rhyme with each picture name.

List Words

fold

rope

road

toe

1. _____

2. _____

3. _____

4. _____

Here are three ways to spell the long **e**
sound: <u>He</u> <u>ea</u>ts b<u>ee</u>ts.

Print the List Word that matches each clue.

List Words

feet

three

we

meal

1. 1, 2, ___, 4

2. something to eat

3. you and I

4. more than one foot

The **ou** sound is spelled two ways: <u>around</u>, <u>how</u>.
Read each word. Print a List Word that has
the opposite meaning.

List Words

found

down

our

out

1. in

2. up

3. lost

4. your

List Words

down
kite
feet
out
eat
found

Print a List Word to complete each sentence.

_____

1. I _____ a dime!

2. We can fly the _____ today.

3. Do not go _____ in this rain.

4. My bike fell _____ .

5. The rope is three _____ long.

6. Ted can _____ this meal with us.

r Blends

Get Ready

Read the sentences.

How now **brown** cow? Have you any jokes?
No? Well, here are a few you might like:
1. What **drink** do you get when you
cross a cow with a jogger?
2. What do you get **from** a cow
at the North Pole?
3. Why don't cows tell jokes?

1. a milkshake
2. cold cream
3. They're always in a bad mooood!

Get Set

Read the sentences again. Say each word in
dark print. Listen for the beginning sounds.

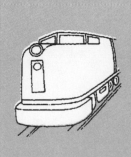
The word **train** begins with the sounds for **t**
and **r.** The letter **r** can form a **blend** when it
follows another letter. What **r** blend sounds do
you hear at the beginning of the words
brown, drink, and **from?**

Go!

Sounds, Letters, and Words

Print the missing letters in each word.
Trace the letters to spell List Words.

1. _____ om   7. _____ ap

2. _____ ow   8. _____ ain

3. _____ own

4. _____ oke

5. _____ ink

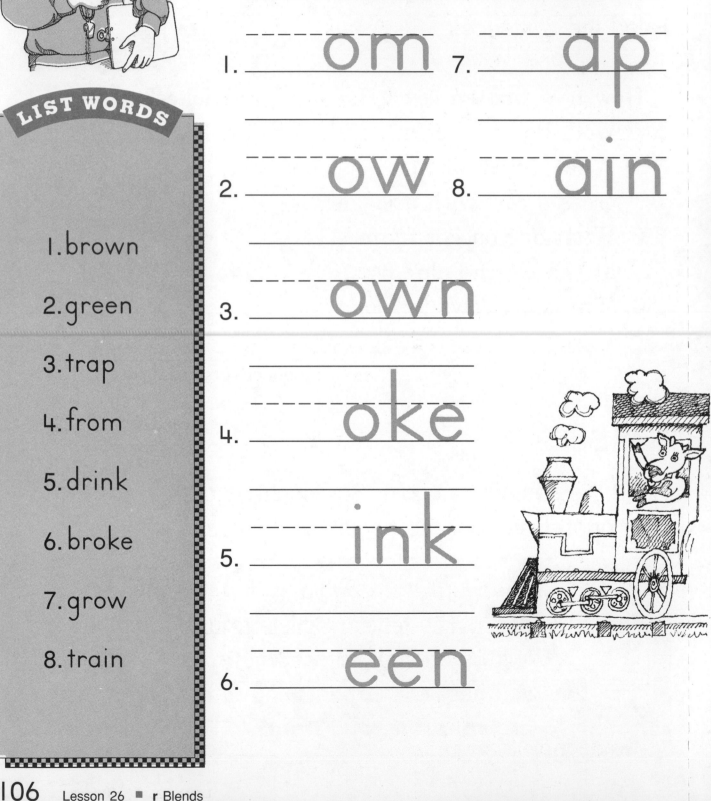

6. _____ een

LIST WORDS

1. brown

2. green

3. trap

4. from

5. drink

6. broke

7. grow

8. train

ABC Order

Print each group of List Words in ABC order.

green   brown   trap

_____   _____   _____

1. _____   _____   _____

drink   broke   from

_____   _____   _____

2. _____   _____   _____

Missing Words

Print a List Word to complete each sentence.

_____

1. The cat _____ the vase.

_____

2. Flowers _____ in the garden.

_____

3. I got a letter _____ Alex.

_____

4. Peter took the _____ to Santa Fe.

List Words

brown	trap	drink	grow
green	from	broke	train

Rhyming Words

Print the List Word that rhymes with the given words.

1. rain   lane

_____

_____

2. nap   strap

_____

_____

3. throw   mow

_____

_____

4. down   frown

_____

_____

5. sink   think

_____

_____

6. bean   seen

_____

_____

Spelling Superstar

Writing

Do you know any jokes? Write a joke for your parents.

l Blends

Get Ready

Read the sentences.

Brrring! Brrring! The alarm **clock** is ringing. It's time to wake up. What time is it? How do you know?

The little **black** hand is on the eight. The big black hand is on the twelve. Wow! Time flies by quickly! Do you know how the monkey made time really **fly?** He threw the clock out the window!

Get Set

Read the sentences again. Say each word in dark print. Listen for the beginning sounds.

The word **clock** begins with the sounds for **c** and **l.** The letter **l** can form a **blend** when it follows another letter. What **l** blend sounds do you hear at the beginning of the words **black** and **fly?**

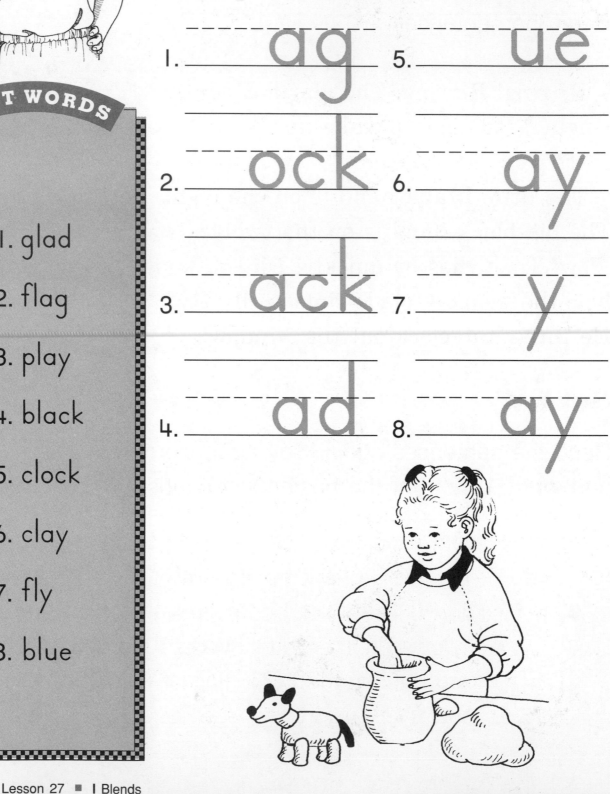

Go!

Sounds, Letters, and Words

Print the missing blends for the words.
Trace the letters to spell List Words.

1. _____ ag

2. _____ ock

3. _____ ack

4. _____ ad

5. _____ ue

6. _____ ay

7. _____ y

8. _____ ay

LIST WORDS

1. glad

2. flag

3. play

4. black

5. clock

6. clay

7. fly

8. blue

Beginning Sounds

Print the List Words that begin with the blends shown.

cl

1. _____

2. _____

fl

3. _____

4. _____

bl

5. _____

6. _____

gl

7. _____

pl

8. _____

Vocabulary

Print a List Word to match each clue.

1. Do this at recess.

_____

2. This is the opposite of white.

_____

3. Make a pot with this.

_____

4. This tells time.

_____

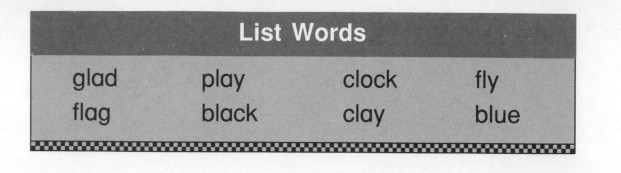

List Words

glad	play	clock	fly
flag	black	clay	blue

Proofreading

Each sentence has two mistakes. Use the proofreading marks to fix each mistake. Write the misspelled List Words on the lines.

Proofreading Marks
⬭ spelling mistake
⊙ add period

1. A flagg flies above my school

_____

_____

_____

2. Its colors are red, white, and bloo

_____

_____

3. It makes me gled to _____ _____
see it fli in the wind. _____ _____

Spelling Superstar

Writing

What is your favorite time of day? Write some sentences that tell what you do at that time.

s Blends

Get Ready

Read the poem.

Whoa!
There they go!
Two feet, one board,
and a big hill of **snow!**
Last ride—no way!
Hey, we could **slide** all day!

Get Set

Read the poem again. Say each word in dark print. Listen for the **s** blends.

The word **slide** begins with the sounds for **s** and **l**. The letter **s** can form a **blend** when it is followed by another letter. What **s** blend sound do you hear at the beginning of the word **snow?** What **s** blend sound do you hear at the end of the word **last?**

Go!

Sounds, Letters, and Words

Print the missing letters for the words.
Trace the letters to spell List Words.

LIST WORDS

1. small
2. last
3. spot
4. slow
5. snow
6. spoon
7. slide
8. star

1. _____ ow
2. _____ all
3. _____ ow
4. _____ ide
5. _____ oon

6. _____ ar
7. _____ la
8. _____ ot

Missing Words

Print List Words to complete the
sentences. The word shapes will help you.

1. A little dot is a ⬜⬜⬜⬜⬜ ⬜⬜⬜⬜ .

2. <u>Low</u> rhymes with ⬜⬜⬜⬜ and ⬜⬜⬜⬜ .

3. Eat your soup with a ⬜⬜⬜⬜⬜ .

4. <u>Ride</u> and <u>hide</u> rhyme with ⬜⬜⬜⬜ .

5. A ⬜⬜⬜⬜ shines in the sky.

6. It rained ⬜⬜⬜⬜ night.

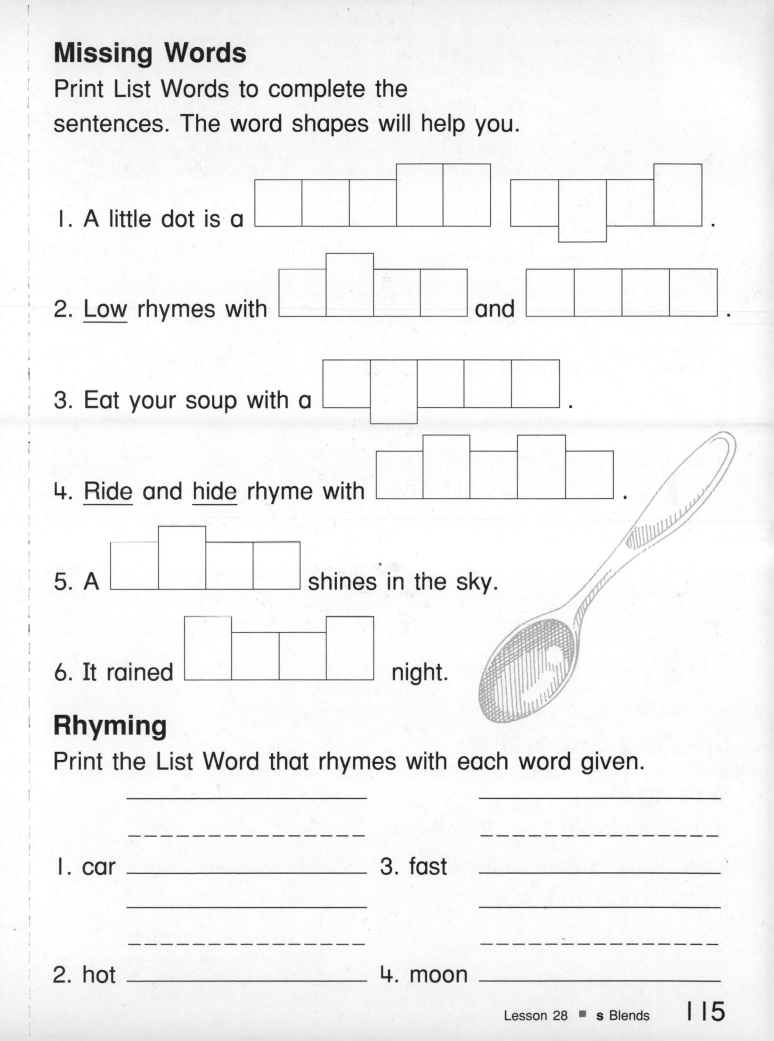

Rhyming

Print the List Word that rhymes with each word given.

1. car _____   3. fast _____

2. hot _____   4. moon _____

Missing Words

Print List Words to finish the story.

_____

I like to play in the _____ . I find a

_____   _____

_____ hill. Then I _____

down it! Sometimes the ride is fast, and sometimes the

_____

ride is _____ .

Spelling Superstar

Writing

Some rides are fast. Some are slow. Write some sentences about a ride you like.

Name _____

y as a Vowel

Get Ready

Read the sentences.

Hey, hey! What do you say?
I could tell knock-knock jokes all **day!**

Knock. Knock.

Who's there?

Boo.

Boo who?

Try not to **cry.**
Knock. Knock.

Go **away!**

Get Set

Read the sentences again. Say each word in dark
print. Listen for the sound the **y** spells in each word.

 The letter **y** spells the long **i** sound in **fly.** You
can hear the long **i** sound in **try** and **cry.**

 The letter **y** helps to spell the long **a** sound in
tray. What vowel sound does **y** help to spell
in **day** and **away?**

Go!

Sounds, Letters, and Words

Print each List Word under its heading.

y helps to spell /ā/

1. _____

2. _____

3. _____

4. _____

y spells /ī/

5. _____

6. _____

7. _____

8. _____

Opposites

Print the List Word that means the opposite of each word.

1. here

_____

- - - - - - - - - - - - - - - -

3. laugh

_____

- - - - - - - - - - - - - - - -

5. night

_____

- - - - - - - - - - - - - - - -

2. we

_____

- - - - - - - - - - - - - - - -

4. your

_____

- - - - - - - - - - - - - - - -

6. earth

_____

- - - - - - - - - - - - - - - -

Ending Sounds

Print the List Words that end with **ay.**

_____

- - - - - - - - - - - - - - - -

1. _____

_____

- - - - - - - - - - - - - - - -

2. _____

_____

- - - - - - - - - - - - - - - -

3. _____

Scrambled Letters

Unscramble the letters. Print the List Words on the lines.

_____

- - - - - - - - - - - - - - - -

1. ryc _____

2. ysk _____

_____

- - - - - - - - - - - - - - - -

3. tyr _____

4. ym _____

List Words

away	try	they	my
pay	sky	cry	day

Proofreading

Each sentence has two mistakes. Use the proofreading marks to fix each mistake. Write the misspelled List Words correctly on the lines.

Proofreading Marks

◯ spelling mistake

≡ capital letter

1. Rosa and john want to tri a new game.

_____

_____

_____

2. at the store, thay picked one to play.

_____

_____

3. aunt Peggy gave them the money to pey for it.

_____

_____

Spelling Superstar

Writing

Suppose one of these visitors knocked on your door. Write some sentences that tell what you would say.

y as a Vowel

Get Ready

Read the poem.

A **baby** dog is called a **puppy,**
and a kitten is a baby cat.
A baby fish is like a guppy.
There's nothing wrong with that!

No matter if it's small or big,
will a piglet **stay** a baby pig?
Even though it's cute and **funny,**
will a baby rabbit stay a bunny?

Get Set

Read the poem again. Say each word in dark
print. Listen for the vowel sound the **y** spells.

 Sometimes the letter **y** has the long **e** sound,
as in **baby, puppy,** and **funny.**

 The letter **y** helps to spell the long **a** sound in
spray. What vowel sound does **y** help to spell
in **stay?**

121

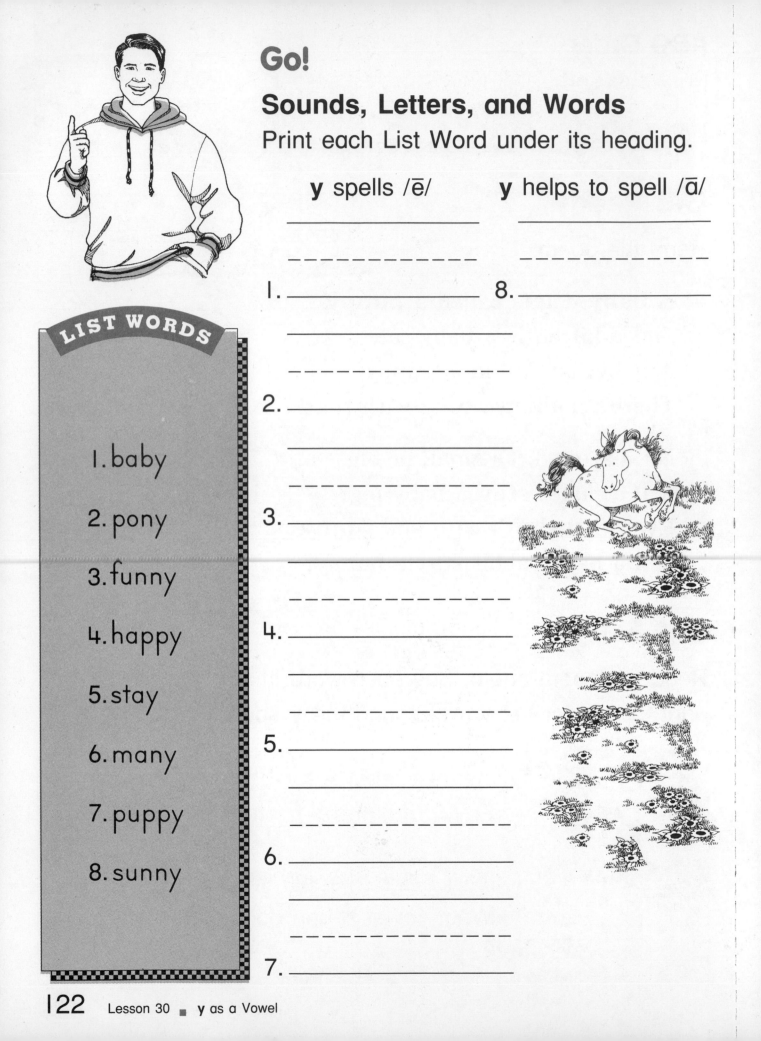

Go!

Sounds, Letters, and Words

Print each List Word under its heading.

y spells /ē/   **y** helps to spell /ā/

1. _____   8. _____

2. _____

3. _____

4. _____

5. _____

6. _____

7. _____

LIST WORDS

1. baby
2. pony
3. funny
4. happy
5. stay
6. many
7. puppy
8. sunny

ABC Order

Print each group of words in ABC order.

puppy   happy   stay

_____   _____   _____

1. _____   _____   _____

baby   many   funny

_____   _____   _____

2. _____   _____   _____

Vocabulary

Print a List Word to match each clue.

1. It's not a big horse.

_____

It's a _____ .

2. It makes you laugh.

_____

It's _____ .

3. It's not cloudy.

_____

It's _____ .

4. It's more than a few.

_____

It's _____ .

5. It's not sad.

_____

It's _____ .

6. It's a baby dog.

_____

It's a _____ .

List Words

funny	baby	many	pony
happy	stay	puppy	sunny

Story Puzzle

Print List Words to finish the story.

_____

_ _ _ _ _ _ _ _ _ _ _ _ _ _ _ _ _

It is a hot, _____ day. Li doesn't

_____

_ _ _ _ _ _ _ _ _ _ _ _ _ _ _ _ _

want to _____ at home. He takes

_____

_ _ _ _ _ _ _ _ _ _ _ _ _ _ _ _ _

his _____ sister to the park. There they ride

_____

_ _ _ _ _ _ _ _ _ _ _ _ _ _ _ _ _

on a _____ .

Spelling Superstar

Writing

A puppy or a kitten need a lot of care.
Write some sentences that tell how
you would take care of a puppy
or kitten.

Instant Replay • Lessons 26–30

Time Out

Now it's time to review what you have learned about words with blends and **y** as a vowel.

Lesson 26

The letter **r** can form a blend when it follows another letter, as in <u>trap</u>.

List Words
from
drink
grow
brown

Unscramble each List Word. Print each word correctly.

1. nirdk

_____

2. rnobw

_____

3. wrog

_____

4. mrfo

_____

Listen for the **l** blend sound at the beginning
of the word <u>black</u>.

List Words

glad
play
blue
clock

Print the List Word that matches each clue.

1. The sky is ____.

_____

_ _ _ _ _ _ _ _ _ _ _ _ _

_____

2. Do this with a
game.

_____

_ _ _ _ _ _ _ _ _ _ _ _ _

_____

3. This tells the time.

_____

_ _ _ _ _ _ _ _ _ _ _ _ _

_____

4. This means to
feel happy.

_____

_ _ _ _ _ _ _ _ _ _ _ _ _

_____

The letter **s** can form a blend at the beginning or
the end of a word, as in <u>small</u> and <u>last</u>.

List Words

slide
spoon
star
snow

Print the List Word that names each picture.

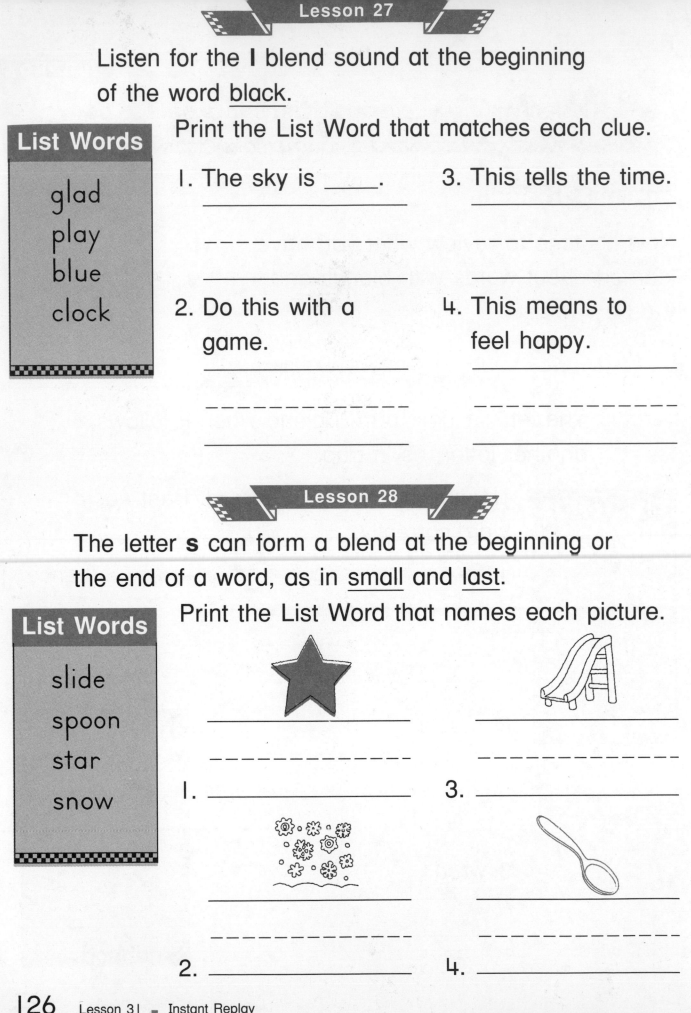

_____

_ _ _ _ _ _ _ _ _ _ _ _ _

1. _____

_____

_ _ _ _ _ _ _ _ _ _ _ _ _

2. _____

_____

_ _ _ _ _ _ _ _ _ _ _ _ _

3. _____

_____

_ _ _ _ _ _ _ _ _ _ _ _ _

4. _____

The letter **y** can help spell the long **a** sound, as in <u>pay</u>. It also spells the long **i** sound, as in <u>sky</u>.

Print List Words that rhyme with each word.

List Words

cry

they

try

away

1. day _____ _____

2. dry _____ _____

Sometimes **y** stands for the long **e** sound, as in many.

It can also help to spell the long **a** sound, as in <u>stay</u>.

Print a List Word to complete each sentence.

List Words

sunny

happy

baby

funny

1. A joke is a _____ story.

2. A puppy is a _____ dog.

3. Today is hot and _____ .

4. I am _____ , not sad.

Fill in the crossword puzzle. Print a List Word to match each clue.

List Words

they

away

brown

play

spoon

baby

ACROSS

2. a very small person

3. you use this at the table

5. not here

DOWN

1. he and she

2. a color

4. have fun

Name _____

LESSON
32

th and wh Words

Get Ready

Read the sentences.

Last summer **when** I went to camp, I didn't go alone. It was a summer camp for families. So my **mother** and **father** went **with** me!

Mother learned to water ski. Father tried to weave a basket from straw, but it looked like a hat! I had lots of fun, especially watching them!

Get Set

Read the sentences again. Say each word in dark print. Listen for the **th** sounds and the **wh** sounds.

 When **w** and **h** come together, they make a new sound, as in the word **whale.** What sound do you hear at the beginning of the word **when?**

 When **t** and **h** come together, they make a new sound, as in the word **bath.** Listen for the **th** sound in the words **mother, father,** and **with.**

Go!

Sounds, Letters, and Words

Print the List Words with the sound **th.**

1. _____

2. _____

3. _____ 4. _____

Print the List Words with the sound **wh.**

5. _____

6. _____

7. _____

8. _____

LIST WORDS

1. where

2. why

3. when

4. mother

5. white

6. father

7. bath

8. with

130   Lesson 32 ■ **th** and **wh** Words

Vocabulary

Print a List Word to match each clue. Use the word shapes.

1. This asks at what time.

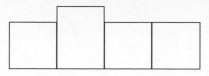

2. This is your dad.

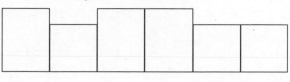

3. This asks in what place.

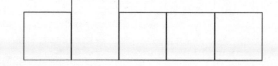

4. This is your mom.

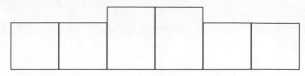

5. This makes you clean.

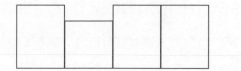

6. This asks for what reason.

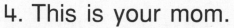

Puzzle

Write the missing List Word in the correct box in the puzzle.

ACROSS

2. ___ do you like camp?
4. I play ___ my cat.
5. ___ is my cap?
6. He is my ___ .

DOWN

1. She is my ___ .
2. ___ will dinner be ready?
3. I have ___ teeth.

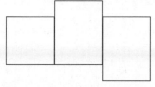
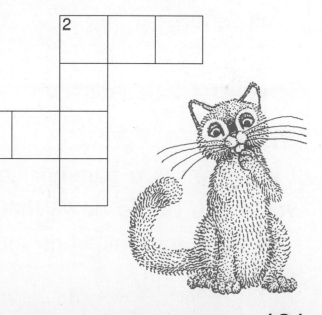

List Words

where	when	white	bath
why	mother	father	with

Proofreading

Each sentence has two mistakes. Use the proofreading marks to fix each mistake. Print the misspelled List Words correctly on the lines.

Proofreading Marks

⬭ spelling mistake

≡ capital letter

1. liz gave our dog Snowball a bathe.

_____

_____

2. she dried his fur weth a towel.

_____

_____

3. Now snowball is wite as snow.

_____

_____

Spelling Superstar

Writing

If you went to a summer camp, what would you like to do? Write some sentences that tell what you would do to have fun.

sh and ch Words

Get Ready

Read the sentences.

The chef will **show** how to make **lunch.**
She will **chop** the vegetables very carefully.
She will cook them so that they taste delicious.
Then she will put them in a **dish** and make
them look beautiful. Her name is Julia Child.

Get Set

Read the sentences again. Say each word in dark
print. Listen for the **sh** sounds and the **ch** sounds.

When **s** and **h** come together they make a
new sound, as in the word **shell.** Listen for
the **sh** sound in the words **show** and **she.**
What sound do you hear at the end of the
word **dish?**

When **c** and **h** come together, they make a
new sound, as in the word **chair.** Listen for
the **ch** sound in the words **chop** and **lunch.**

Go!

Sounds, Letters, and Words

Print the missing letters for each word.
Trace the letters to spell List Words.

1. di_____

2. lun_____

3. _____he

4. _____ow

5. c_____p

6. _____oe

7. _____ild

8. s_____p

LIST WORDS

1. chop

2. child

3. lunch

4. she

5. dish

6. show

7. shop

8. shoe

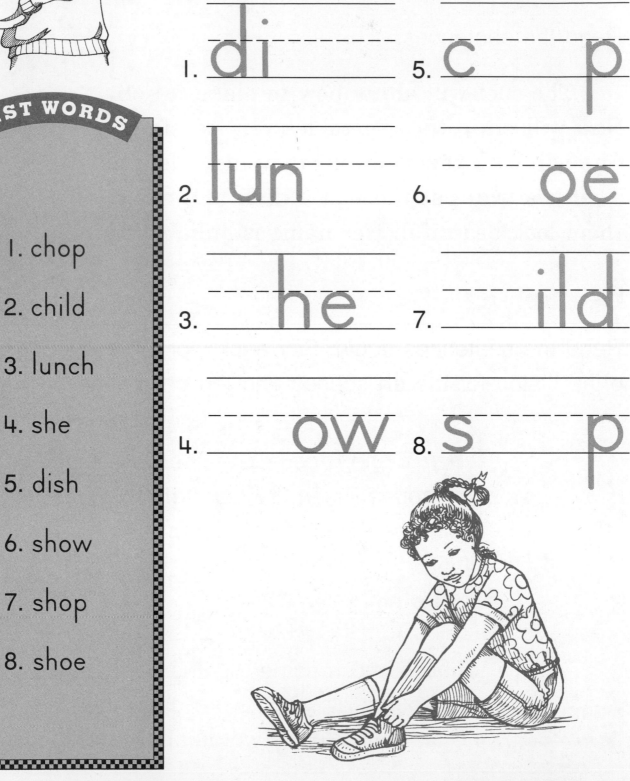

Rhyming

Print the List Word that rhymes with each word given.

1. wish

   _____

   ----

2. he

   _____

   ----

3. blow

   _____

   ----

4. crunch

   _____

   ----

5. glue

   _____

   ----

6. wild

   _____

Scrambled Letters

Unscramble each List Word. Print the correct word on the line. The word shapes will help you.

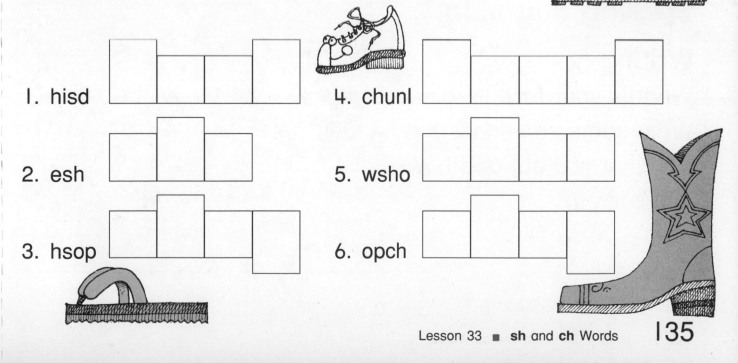

1. hisd

2. esh

3. hsop

4. chunl

5. wsho

6. opch

List Words

chop	lunch	dish	shop
child	she	show	shoe

Puzzle

Fill in the crossword puzzle. Print a
List Word to match each clue.

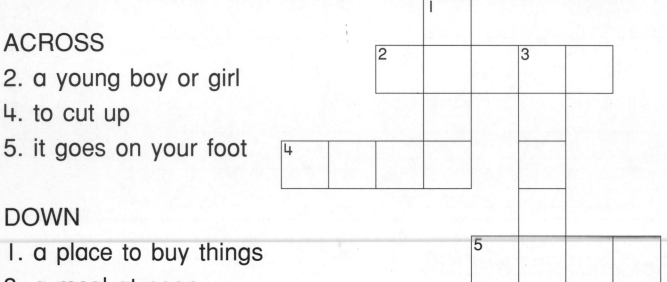

ACROSS

2. a young boy or girl
4. to cut up
5. it goes on your foot

DOWN

1. a place to buy things
3. a meal at noon

Spelling Superstar

Writing

What is your favorite dinner?
Write some sentences that
tell what you eat and how
it is served.

Name _____

Adding <u>ed</u> to Action Words

Get Ready

Read the sentences.

Dinosaurs lived millions of years ago. Some of these creatures **looked** like giant lizards. The biggest was Tyrannosaurus Rex. Rex was bigger than a house! He **needed** a lot of space to roam around. Rex liked plants, but he also **wanted** to eat meat. The other animals usually stayed out of his way!

Get Set

Read the sentences again. Look at the words in dark print. To make an action word tell what has already happened, you can add the ending **ed.**

The word **cooked** tells about something that already happened. It ends with the sound for **ed.** Listen for the sounds at the end of the words **looked, needed,** and **wanted.** Do those words tell what has already happened?

137

Go!

Sounds, Letters, and Words

Add the letters **ed** to each word. Trace the letters to spell List Words.

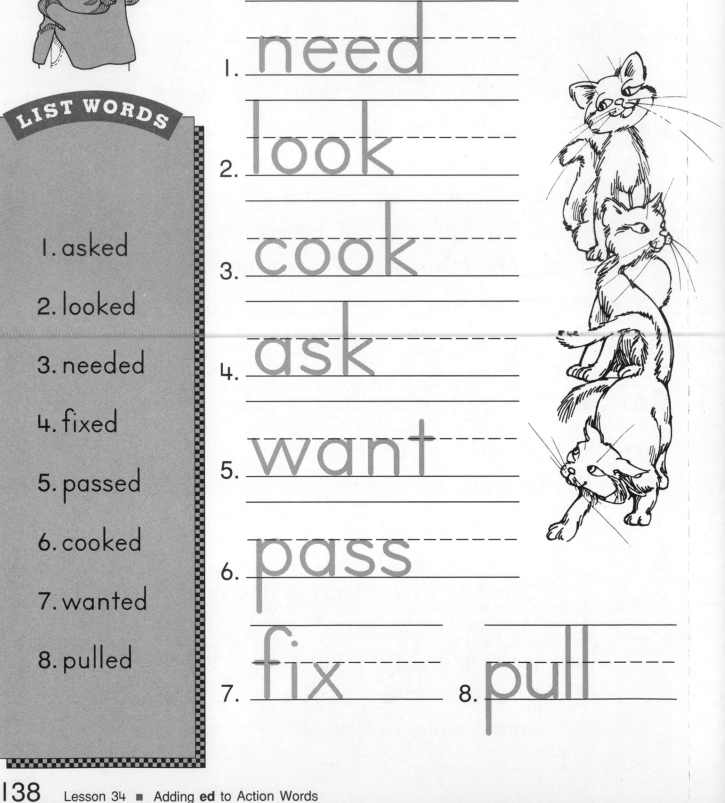

1. need
2. look
3. cook
4. ask
5. want
6. pass
7. fix
8. pull

ABC Order

Print each group of List Words in ABC order.

| asked |
| looked |
| passed |
| fixed |

1. _____

2. _____

3. _____

4. _____

| needed |
| cooked |
| wanted |
| pulled |

5. _____

6. _____

7. _____

8. _____

Vocabulary

Print the List Word that has the same meaning.

1. baked

_____

2. invited

_____

3. went by

_____

4. wished

_____

5. had to have

_____

Proofreading

Each sentence has two mistakes. Use the proofreading marks to fix each mistake. Print the misspelled List Words correctly on the lines.

Proofreading Marks

⬭ spelling mistake

⊙ add period

1. Tom pulld his wagon home

_____

_____

2. Dad lookt at Tom's wagon

_____

_____

3. Then Dad fixt the flat tire

_____

Spelling Superstar

Writing

Tyrannosaurus Rex was very big. What other big animals can you think of? Write a description of one of them.

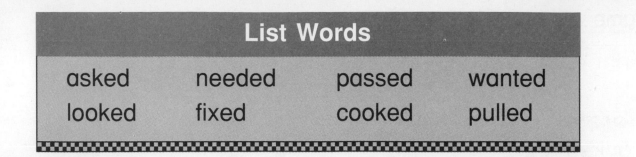

Adding ing to Action Words

Get Ready

Read the poem.

A breeze is **blowing.**
The stream is flowing.
There's no school today,
  and we're **going rowing.**
Having fun all day long,
  we'll be **singing** a song.
So why don't you come along?

Get Set

Read the poem again. Look at the words in dark print. To make an action word tell what is going on now, you can add the ending **ing.**

The word **rowing** tells about something that is going on now. It ends with the sound for **ing.** Listen for the sounds at the end of the words **blowing, going, having,** and **singing.** Do those words tell what is going on now?

141

Go!

Sounds, Letters, and Words

Print the missing ending for each word.
Trace the letters to spell List Words.

LIST WORDS

1. doing
2. singing
3. being
4. blowing
5. rowing
6. having
7. going
8. sleeping

1. sleep
2. blow
3. sing
4. row
5. hav
6. do
7. be
8. go

Vocabulary

Print the correct List Words for the words in dark print.

1. Dad is **row** the boat.

_____

2. They are **have** fun.

_____

3. I am **blow** a bubble.

_____

4. He is **sing** a song.

_____

5. She is **do** her homework.

_____

6. The baby is **sleep.**

_____

7. The dog is **be** playful.

_____

8. We are **go** to a movie.

_____

ABC Order

Print these List Words in ABC order.

sleeping	going
rowing	blowing

1. _____

2. _____

3. _____

4. _____

List Words

doing	being	rowing	going
singing	blowing	having	sleeping

Missing Words

Print List Words to complete the sentences.

1. Anita is _____ her homework.

2. Paul is _____ fun

_____ a song.

3. Lucy is _____ silly.

Spelling Superstar

Writing

Holidays are fun, but so is school. Write to your teacher. Tell what you like about school.

Dear Teacher,

Instant Replay • Lessons 32–35

Time Out

Take another look at the sounds **th** and **wh, sh** and **ch,** and adding **ed** or **ing** to action words.

Lesson 32

When **t** and **h** come together, they make a new sound, as in the word <u>father</u>. When **w** and **h** come together, they make a new sound, as in the word <u>why</u>.

List Words
mother
when
bath
white

Finish the story. Print a List Word in each blank. You may have to use a capital letter.

_____

_____

_____ it is time for bed,

_____

_____

I first take a _____ . Then I

_____

brush my _____ teeth. Then I

_____

kiss my _____ good night.

145

You can hear the sound that **s** and **h** make together in the word **show.** Listen to the sound that **c** and **h** make together in the word **chop.** Print a List Word for each clue.

List Words

child
dish
lunch
shoe

I am thinking of a word that begins like . . .

1. _____

2. _____

3. _____

4. _____

Add **ed** to make an action word tell what has already happened: **jump** + **ed** = **jumped.**

List Words

asked
cooked
fixed
pulled

Add the ending **ed** to make List Words.

fix

1. _____

ask

2. _____

pull

3. _____

cook

4. _____

To tell about what is going on now, add **ing** to an action word: **go** + **ing** = **going.**

Print a List Word to tell what is going on in each picture.

List Words

rowing
sleeping
singing
blowing

1. _____

2. _____

3. _____

4. _____

List Words

when
mother
dish
child
fixed
needed
rowing
singing

Solve the crossword puzzle. Print a List Word to match each clue.

ACROSS

4. another name for <u>Mom</u>
5. making musical sounds
7. repaired
8. a young person

DOWN

1. asks at what time
2. making a boat go
3. something to put food on
6. had to have

Writing and Proofreading Guide

Name each picture. Print each List Word that begins
with the same sound as the picture name.

1. Choose something to write about.
2. Write your ideas. Don't worry about
   making mistakes.
3. Now proofread your work.
   Use these proofreading marks to check your work.

Proofreading Marks
- ⬭ spelling mistake
- ☰ capital letter
- ⊙ add period

we have a new (pupy) at   home⊙
‗‗

4. Make your final copy.

   We have a new puppy at home.

5. Share your writing.

Spelling Workout Dictionary

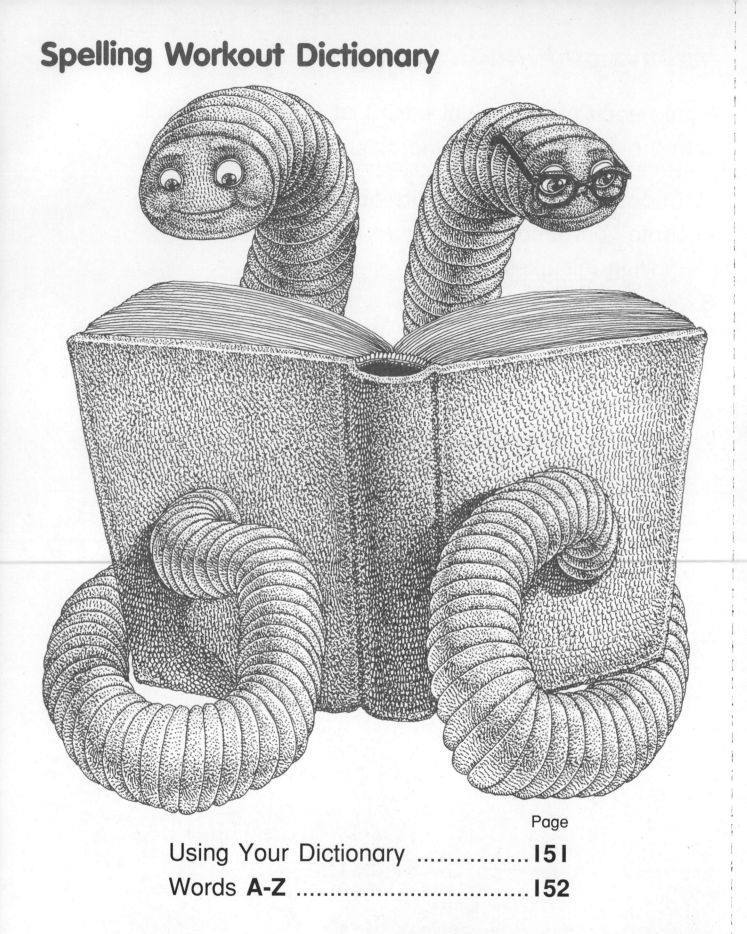

Using Your Dictionary

The Spelling Workout Dictionary shows
you many things about your spelling
words.

The **entry word** listed in
ABC order is the word
you are looking up.

The **definition** tells us
what the word means.

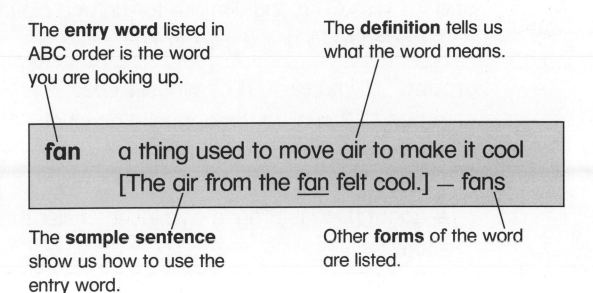

fan　a thing used to move air to make it cool
[The air from the <u>fan</u> felt cool.] — fans

The **sample sentence**
show us how to use the
entry word.

Other **forms** of the word
are listed.

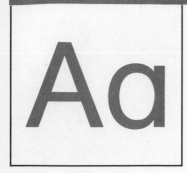

age   the time that a person or thing has existed from birth or beginning [Jan started school at the <u>age</u> of five.] —**ages**

and   **1** also [Tim <u>and</u> Jim like to run <u>and</u> play.] **2** added to [5 <u>and</u> 2 equals 7.]

around   **1** in a circle [The wheel turned <u>around</u>.] **2** in or to the opposite direction [We turned <u>around</u> and went back home.] **3** on all sides of [The flowers grew <u>around</u> the lake.] **4** about [Dad is <u>around</u> two inches taller than Mom.]

ask   **1** to use words to find out [I will <u>ask</u> her what her name is.] **2** to invite [Tom will <u>ask</u> Mike to his party.] —**asks, asked, asking**

attic

attic   the room or space below the roof of a house [They found a box of old books in the <u>attic</u>.]

away   **1** to another place [The child ran <u>away</u> from the strange dog.] **2** in the proper place [Please put your toys <u>away</u>.] **3** not here [My sister is <u>away</u> today.]

ax   a tool for chopping or splitting wood [Dad chopped the firewood with an <u>ax</u>.] —**axes**

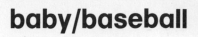

baby a very young child [The <u>baby</u> cried for his bottle.] —**babies**

bag paper, or other soft material made to carry things [I carry my lunch in a <u>bag</u>.] —**bags**

bake to cook by dry heat [We will <u>bake</u> the cake in the oven for 30 minutes.] —**bakes, baked, baking**

balloon **l** a large bag that floats when filled with a gas that is lighter than air [We saw the hot air <u>balloon</u> float across the sky.] **2** a rubber toy that can be blown up with air or gas [The clown gave us a <u>balloon</u> tied to a string.] —**balloons**

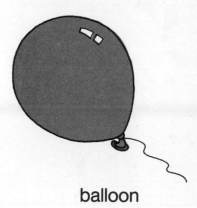

balloon

bark¹ the outside covering of the trunk and branches of a tree [The thick, black <u>bark</u> covered the logs.]

bark² to make the sharp cry of a dog [The dog will <u>bark</u> at the stranger.] —**barks, barked, barking**

barn a farm building for animals or machines [The cows slept in the <u>barn</u>.] —**barns**

barn

baseball a game played with a ball and bat [The children played <u>baseball</u> in the summer.]

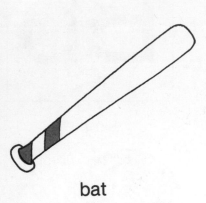

bat

bat¹ **I** a wooden club used in hitting the ball in baseball [Ryan hit the ball with a wooden bat.] **2** to hit with a bat [She will bat the ball over the fence.] —**bats, batted, batting**

bat² an animal that looks like a mouse but with wings of stretched skin [The bat flew out of the barn.] —**bats**

bath **I** the washing of something in water [We gave the dog a bath.] **2** the water used for bathing [The bath was too hot.] —**baths**

being **I** to be now [The baby is being quiet.] **2** a person [A human being is the smartest animal on earth.] —**beings**

best above all others in worth or ability [Laura is the best player on the team.]

big large [New York is a big city.] —**bigger, biggest**

bike

bike a toy to ride that has two wheels and two foot pedals [Ned rode his bike home.] —**bikes**

black the opposite color of white [The night sky was very black.]

blimp an egg-shaped airship [The blimp floated over the football field.] —**blimps**

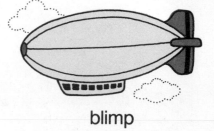

blimp

blow 1 to move air out of the mouth [It is hard to blow up some balloons.] 2 to force air into to clear [I have to blow my nose.] 3 to make a sound by blowing [Did you hear the trumpet blow?] —**blows, blew, blown, blowing**

blue 1 the color of the sky [The blue sky had fluffy, white clouds.] 2 sad [I felt blue when Dad left.] —**bluer, bluest**

boat a small vessel for traveling on water [Lucy sailed the boat across the lake.] —**boats**

bold ready to take risks or face danger; fearless [Columbus was a bold explorer.]

book pages put together with a cover on the outside [It's fun to read a good book.] —**books**

both two [Both babies are crying.]

box a container made of cardboard or wood [Sam keeps his baseball cards in a box.]

branch

branch   part of a tree that grows from the trunk [A bird made a nest on the tree's top <u>branch</u>.] —**branches**

bridge   something built over land or water to serve as a road across [The train crossed the <u>bridge</u> over the river.] —**bridges**

broke   cracked into pieces [Abby <u>broke</u> the vase.] —**broken**

brown   the color of chocolate or coffee [The tree's bark was <u>brown</u>.]

bus   a large motor coach for carrying many passengers [Ed rode the <u>bus</u> to work.] —**buses**

butterfly

but   except [All the girls <u>but</u> Sara like to jump rope.]

butterfly   a brightly colored insect with wide wings [The caterpillar turned into a pretty <u>butterfly</u>.] —**butterflies**

buy   to get by paying money [I will <u>buy</u> a new pencil with this coin.] —**buys, bought, buying**

came   moved from there to here [The cat <u>came</u> to eat.]

can[1]   is able to [<u>Can</u> a wish on a star come true?]

can[2]   a metal container [The tin <u>can</u> was full of peas.] —**cans**

car   anything that moves on wheels [Ron will park his <u>car</u> on the street.] —**cars**

carry   to take from one place to another [I <u>carry</u> books to school.] —**carries, carried, carrying**

cat   a pet with soft fur [My <u>cat</u> likes to play with yarn.] —**cats**

cat

cent   a coin worth a penny [What can I buy with one <u>cent</u>?] —**cents**

child   a young boy or girl [The <u>child</u> will play with that toy.] —**children**

chipmunk   a small squirrel of North America that lives in a hole in the ground [They saw a <u>chipmunk</u> at the park.] —**chipmunks**

chop   to cut with a sharp tool [Mom will <u>chop</u> the nuts with a knife.] —**chops, chopped, chopping**

clock

clay stiff, sticky earth that gets hard when it is baked [We made <u>clay</u> pots in art class.]

clean **1** without dirt [The car is shiny and <u>clean</u>.] **2** to make clean [Please <u>clean</u> your room.] —**cleaner, cleanest; cleans, cleaned, cleaning**

clock a tool used to measure time [Su Lin looked at the <u>clock</u> to see if it was time to go.] —**clocks**

coat

coat an outer garment with sleeves that opens down the front [Kim's hat and gloves match her new <u>coat</u>.] —**coats**

cold **1** chilly, not warm [A <u>cold</u> ice cream cone is good to eat on a hot day.] **2** an illness with sneezing, coughing, and a runny nose [Todd had a <u>cold</u> for a week.] —**colder, coldest, colds**

cook to heat, boil, bake, or roast food [I like to <u>cook</u> hot dogs for lunch.] —**cooks, cooked, cooking**

coop

coop a cage or pen for small animals [The hens were kept in a chicken <u>coop</u>.] —**coops**

cross   to go from one side to the other of
[Amy and Joe <u>cross</u> the street.] —**crosses,
crossed, crossing**

cry   **1** to sob and shed tears when sad or in
pain [Al tried not to <u>cry</u> when he got hurt.]
2 to say loudly [<u>Cry</u> for help if you need me.]
—**cries, cried, crying**

cub   a young bear or lion [The lion <u>cub</u> is very
cute.] —**cubs**

cut   to make an opening with a sharp tool
[I <u>cut</u> the paper with scissors.] —**cuts,
cut, cutting**

day   **1** the time when it is light outside [Owls
sleep during the <u>day</u>.] **2** the 24 hours from
midnight to midnight [What <u>day</u> is your
party?] —**days**

den   **1** a cave or home for animals [The fox hid
in his <u>den</u>.] **2** a small, cozy room [Ana likes
to read in the <u>den</u>.] —**dens**

did   has done [Max <u>did</u> his homework.]

dime   a coin worth ten cents [I will trade this
<u>dime</u> for two nickels.] —**dimes**

den

dog

dish   a plate or bowl used for food [I will put the meat on a clean <u>dish</u>.] —**dishes**

do   to work at [How long will it take you to <u>do</u> your homework?] —**does, did, done, doing**

doe   the female deer [The <u>doe</u> cared for her baby deer.] —**doe or does**

dog   a pet that can look like a fox or wolf [The little <u>dog</u> had a loud bark.] —**dogs**

down   to a lower place [The ball rolled <u>down</u> the hill.]

drink   to swallow a liquid [Don't <u>drink</u> the dirty water.] —**drinks, drank, drunk, drinking**

drop   to fall or let fall [Do not <u>drop</u> your coat on the floor.] —**drops, dropped, dropping**

drum   a musical instrument that is played by beating with sticks or the hands [Meg plays the <u>drum</u> in the school band.] —**drums**

dry   I not wet [The clothes are <u>dry</u> now.] **2** to make or become dry [Please <u>dry</u> the dishes.] —**drier, driest; dries, dried, drying**

duck

duck[1]   a bird with a flat bill and webbed feet [The <u>duck</u> quacked at us.] —**ducks**

duck²   to lower the head quickly [Duck if the ball comes this way.] —**ducks, ducked, ducking**

eat   to take in, chew, and swallow food [We will eat fruit for a snack.] —**eats, ate, eaten, eating**

egg   an oval shape that holds a baby bird until it is ready to be born [The hen laid one egg.] —**eggs**

end   **I** the last or farthest part [Gary went to sleep at the end of the day.] **2** to stop [When will the game end?] —**ends, ended, ending**

family   a group of people who are related [There are six children in Lana's family.] —**families**

fan   a thing used to move air to make it cool [The air from the fan felt cool.] —**fans**

fat   very plump [What a fat puppy!] —**fatter, fattest**

father   a man who has a child [The father took his son fishing.] —**fathers**

feather   one of the soft parts that cover birds [The parrot lost a green feather.] —**feathers**

feet   I parts of the body at the end of one's legs used to stand on [Lisa wore shoes on her feet.] **2** more than one set of twelve inches [A yardstick is three feet long.]

fence   a wall of wood or wire put around a yard [Our yard has a white fence.] —**fences**

fill   to make something full [John will fill the pail with water.] —**fills, filled, filling**

firefly   a small beetle whose lower body glows [The light of the firefly blinks off and on al night.] —**fireflies**

fish   an animal with fins and gills that lives in water [Fish swim in the lake.]

five   the number after four [I have five fingers on each hand.]

fix   to make something right [Dad tried to fix the broken bike.] —**fixes, fixed, fixing**

flag   a cloth with colors or pictures on it [We waved a red, white, and blue flag.] —**flags**

fish

flag

flashlight   an electric light that uses batteries and is small enough to carry [Sal used a flashlight to see into the cave.] —**flashlights**

fly[1]   to move in the air with wings [I saw the bird fly away.] —**flies, flew, flown, flying**

fly[2]   a tiny insect [The fly came in when James went out.] —**flies**

fold   to bend one part of a thing over another part [I will fold the paper in half.] —**folds, folded, folding**

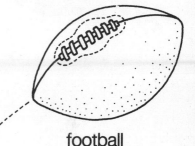

football

follow   to come or go after [The dog wanted to follow me.] —**follows, followed, following**

food   a thing we eat to live and grow [The food was cooked on the stove.] —**foods**

football   a game played with an oval ball [Jan will kick the football over the goal.]

found   got by looking [Pete found a dime.]

fox   a wild animal that has pointed ears and a bushy tail [The fox lives in a den.] —**foxes**

freeze   to harden into ice [The lakes freeze in winter.] —**freezes, froze, freezing**

frog

frog   a small pond animal that hops or makes a croaking sound [The tadpole grew into a frog.] —**frogs**

from   1 starting at [The store is open from nine until five.] 2 out of [Take your coat from the closet.] 3 sent by [She got a gift from me.]

frown   to show that one does not like something [My parents frown when I am late.] —**frowns, frowned, frowning**

fun   a happy time [We had fun at the party.]

funny   makes one laugh [The funny clown had a red nose.] —**funnier, funniest**

game   a form of play [We like the game of hide-and-seek.] —**games**

gave   handed over [I gave the book to him.]

girl   a female child [That girl is my sister.] —**girls**

glad   happy [I am glad that you like me.] —**gladder, gladdest**

glass   a hard substance that breaks easily and lets light through [The window is made of glass.] —**glasses**

go   to move from one place to another [Becky will go home at six.] —**goes, went, gone, going**

got   came to own [Fred got a new bike.]

gray   1 a color made by mixing black and white [The cat had gray fur. 2 to be dark or dull [The gray clouds will bring rain.]

great   very important [She is a great pianist.] —**greater, greatest**

green   the color of grass [Fran painted the room green.]

grin   to give a big smile [The clown made the children grin.] —**grins, grinned, grinning**

ground   land; earth [Mike planted a flower in the ground.]

grow   to get larger or older [The child will grow taller next year.] —**grows, grew, grown, growing**

hand   part of the body at the end of one's arm [I am holding a coin in my hand.] —**hands**

happy   glad [I am happy to see you!] —**happier, happiest**

Hh

hat

has owns or holds [That camel <u>has</u> two humps.] —**have, had, having**

hat a thing used to cover the head [Dan put a <u>hat</u> on his head to keep warm.] —**hats**

have own or hold [I <u>have</u> red hair.] —**has, had, having**

hay grass or clover that is cut and dried for use as food for animals [Horses eat <u>hay</u>.]

heat hot air that can be felt [The <u>heat</u> of the fire made us warm.]

hide to put or keep out of sight [<u>Hide</u> the present in the closet.] —**hides, hid, hiding**

him the form of HE that is used as the object of a verb or preposition [The dog jumped on <u>him</u>.]

hit to bump or knock [The car <u>hit</u> the tree.] —**hits, hit, hitting**

home the place where one lives [Matt's <u>home</u> is on Front Street.] —**homes**

hook curved metal that will catch or hold something [I hung my coat on a <u>hook</u>.] —**hooks**

hop to move in short jumps [The frog will <u>hop</u> into the pond.] —**hops, hopped, hopping**

hopscotch a game where children hop from one space to another [<u>Hopscotch</u> squares were on the sidewalk.]

hot very warm [I burned my hand on the <u>hot</u> stove.] —**hotter, hottest**

house a building where one lives [We will play at Molly's <u>house</u>.] —**houses**

how in what way [<u>How</u> did you get home?]

hug to hold close in a loving way [I will <u>hug</u> my teddy bear.] —**hugs, hugged, hugging**

hunt to try to find [I had to <u>hunt</u> for my homework.] —**hunts, hunted, hunting**

---

ice water frozen solid [Vicky skated on the <u>ice</u>.]

jar a wide glass container [The lid on the jam jar was open.] —**jars**

jet a fast airplane [The jet made a white trail in the sky.] —**jets**

job any work one has to do [My job is to take out the trash.] —**jobs**

jog to run slowly [Paul will jog in the park.] —**jogs, jogged, jogging**

joke a funny story [The joke made me laugh.] —**jokes**

July the seventh month of the year [We go to the beach in July.]

jump to leap [Laura had to jump to get the ball.] —**jumps, jumped, jumping**

just 1 only [I am just being silly.] 2 by a small amount [You just missed a phone call.]

kick to strike with the foot [Kick the ball.] — **kicks, kicked, kicking**

kite a toy that flies in the wind [Fly your kite on a windy day.] —**kites**

ladybug   a small spotted beetle [A <u>ladybug</u> can be red with black spots.] —**ladybugs**

lamp   a thing that gives light [The <u>lamp</u> lit our bedroom.] —**lamps**

last   after all others [Maria was the <u>last</u> one in line.]

late   happening or coming after the usual or expected time [Jody was <u>late</u> for school.] —**later, latest**

ladybug

leg   part of the body used for standing [Jeff's <u>legs</u> hurt from running.] —**legs**

like   to enjoy [June <u>likes</u> dogs.] —**likes, liked, liking**

lock   to fasten a door or safe. We <u>lock</u> our doors at night.] —**locks, locked, locking**

log   a section of a tree that has been cut [Dad put a <u>log</u> in the fire.] —**logs**

look   to see with one's eyes [Carlos will <u>look</u> at the nice sunset.] —**looks, looked, looking**

lot   very much [Grace felt a <u>lot</u> happier when she saw her lost pet.]

luck

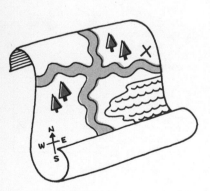

map

luck   good or bad things that seem to happen by chance [It was good <u>luck</u> that I won.]

lunch   a small meal eaten a few hours after breakfast [We like to eat <u>lunch</u> at noon.] —**lunches**

make   to bring into being [Mom will <u>make</u> lunch for us.] —**makes, made, making**

man   an adult male [The <u>man</u> you met is my father.] —**men**

many   a large number of [She read <u>many</u> books about dogs.] —**more, most**

map   a drawing that shows where different places are [We used a <u>map</u> to find our way to Pete's home.] —**maps**

mask   something worn over the face [Kathy wore a scary Halloween <u>mask</u>.] —**masks**

maybe   perhaps [<u>Maybe</u> we can go to the park tomorrow.]

meal   breakfast, lunch, or dinner [Lunch is Bob's favorite <u>meal</u>.] —**meals**

milk   something white to drink that comes from cows [The cow's <u>milk</u> was sweet.]

mine   something that belongs to me [The pen you found is <u>mine</u>.]

mix   to stir or join together [Let's <u>mix</u> nuts into the cookie batter.] —**mixes, mixed, mixing**

mother   a woman who has a child [The <u>mother</u> loves her baby.] —**mothers**

mouse   a small animal found in houses and fields [The <u>mouse</u> ran from the cat.] —**mice**

mouse

mud   wet earth that is soft and sticky [The dog rolled in the <u>mud</u>.]

my   of me [<u>My</u> house is on First Street.]

name   a word for a person, place, or thing [My friend's <u>name</u> is Mary Pate.] —**names**

neat   clean and tidy [Dale keeps his room <u>neat</u>.] —**neater, neatest**

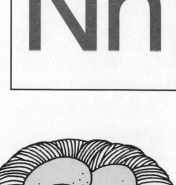

Nn

neck   the part that joins the head to the body [She wore a scarf around her <u>neck</u>.] —**necks**

need   to want [I <u>need</u> a stamp to mail this letter.] —**needs, needed, needing**

nest

nest   a home made by a bird [The robin's eggs were in the <u>nest</u>.] —**nests**

171

not   in no way [My mom was <u>not</u> happy to see the mud on my feet.]

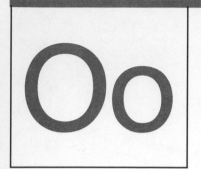

off   not on [Take your hat <u>off</u> and put it on the hook.]

one   the number before two [You may eat only <u>one</u> piece of cheese at a time.]

ouch   a sound made to show sudden pain [When he fell, he cried, "<u>Ouch!</u>"]

our   the one that belongs to us [We will paint the trim on <u>our</u> house red.]

out   away from the inside [Cathy will take the dog <u>out</u> for a walk.]

owl   a bird with large eyes, large head, a short beak, and sharp claws [The <u>owl</u> hunts at night.] —**owls**

pass   1 go by [We <u>pass</u> your house each day.] 2 to move [Please <u>pass</u> the bread to me.] —**passes, passed, passing**

paste   a mixture of flour and water that is used for sticking things together [Barbara used <u>paste</u> to put her photos in the book.]

pay   to give money for something [Did you <u>pay</u> for the paper?] —**pays, paid, paying**

pen   a tool used to write with ink [We write with a <u>pen</u> in fifth grade.] —**pens**

pen

penny   a coin worth one cent [Cora put the shiny, new <u>penny</u> in her bank.] —**pennies**

pick   to choose or select [The judge will <u>pick</u> the winner.] —**picks, picked, picking**

pig   a farm animal raised for its meat [The <u>pig</u> had pink skin and a short tail.] —**pigs**

pig

pill   a tablet of medicine [Joan gave the sick dog a <u>pill</u>.] —**pills**

pin   a stiff, pointed wire used to hold things together [We put our name tags on with a <u>pin</u>.] —**pins**

pipe   a long tube through which a liquid can flow [The water flowed through a <u>pipe</u>.] —**pipes**

place   **1** a space or spot [This is a good <u>place</u> to rest.] **2** to put somewhere [<u>Place</u> the pencil on the desk.] —**places, placed, placing**

plane an aircraft [The <u>plane</u> flew above the clouds.] —**planes**

plane

play to have fun [It is fun to <u>play</u> baseball.] —**plays, played, playing**

pond a small lake [The cows drank from the <u>pond</u>.] —**ponds**

pony a type of small horse [We rode on a <u>pony</u> at the fair.] —**ponies**

pop **1** a short, loud sound [We heard a <u>pop</u> when the balloon broke.] **2** sweet soda drink [I like to drink cherry <u>pop</u>.] —**pops**

pot a round container used for cooking or holding things [Dad cooked the soup in a <u>pot</u>.] —**pots**

pull to move something nearer [The boy must <u>pull</u> his sled up the hill.] —**pulls, pulled, pulling**

puppet a small figure moved by strings or the hands [Alicia made the <u>puppet</u> dance.] —**puppets**

pup, puppy a young dog [The little <u>puppy</u> barked and jumped.] —**puppies**

push   to press against so as to move [I had to
push my bike up the hill.] —**pushes,
pushed, pushing**

queen   a woman who rules a country [The
queen wears a gold crown.] —**queens**

quick   done with speed [We made a quick trip
to the store.]

ran   moved very fast [The dog ran after the
ball.]

red   the color of blood [I ate a red apple.]
—**redder, reddest**

rest   to keep still [The baby will rest in the crib.]
—**rests, rested, resting**

ride   to sit on and move [Beth will ride in the
car.] —**rides, rode, ridden, riding**

ring¹   I to make the sound of a bell [The
phone will ring.] **2** to cause a bell to sound
[Ring the doorbell.] —**rings, rang, ringing**

ring²   a thin band shaped like a circle and worn
on a finger [Nina wore a silver ring.] —**rings**

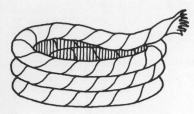

rope

road   a way for cars and trucks to go from place to place [The dirt <u>road</u> was bumpy.] —**roads**

rock   a large stone [I sat on the <u>rock</u>.] —**rocks**

rope   a thick cord [Keisha tied a <u>rope</u> to the tree.] —**ropes**

row[1]   people or things in a line [Juan sits in the first <u>row</u>.] —**rows**

row[2]   to move a boat using oars [Debbie had to <u>row</u> the boat to shore.] —**rows, rowed, rowing**

rowboat

rowboat   a boat that uses oars to move [Don used oars to move the <u>rowboat</u> across the pond.] —**rowboats**

rug   a thing that covers floors [The <u>rug</u> kept the floor clean.] —**rugs**

run   to move with the legs very fast [Sara had to <u>run</u> to catch the bus.] —**runs, ran, run, running**

seal   a sea animal with four flippers [The <u>seal</u> swam underwater.] —**seals**

see   to look at [Did you <u>see</u> me in the window?] —**sees, saw, seen, seeing**

set   to put in a certain place or position [Beth <u>set</u> the book on the table.] —**sets, set, setting**

seven   the number after six [There are <u>seven</u> days in a week.]

she   a girl or woman being talked about [Liz said that <u>she</u> found a key.]

sheep

sheep   a farm animal that is covered with wool [A lamb is a baby <u>sheep</u>.]

shell   a hard covering [I found a snail's <u>shell</u> on the beach.] —**shells**

shirt   a thing to wear on top of the body [Dad wore a <u>shirt</u> and tie.] —**shirts**

shirt

shoe   a cover for the foot [My <u>shoe</u> is made of leather.] —**shoes**

shop   to go to the store to buy something [Jean must <u>shop</u> for a new coat.] —**shops, shopped, shopping**

shoe

should   a helping verb used to speak of something that one ought to do [We <u>should</u> always do our homework.]

show   to let a person see something [Will you <u>show</u> us your new dress?] —**shows, showed, shown, showing**

sing   to make music with the voice [She can <u>sing</u> very well.] —**sings, sang, sung, singing**

sit   to bend at the waist to rest on one's bottom [We must <u>sit</u> down all day at school.] —**sits, sat, sitting**

six   the number after five [There are <u>six</u> months in half a year.]

sky   the air above the earth [We could see clouds floating in the blue <u>sky</u>.] —**skies**

sled   a low platform on runners, used for riding over the snow [Paula zoomed down the hill on her <u>sled</u>.] —**sleds**

sleep   to close one's eyes and rest [Paulo can <u>sleep</u> only if it is dark.] —**sleeps, slept, sleeping**

slide   a playground toy with a long, slanted board [Lynn likes to go down the slide.] —**slides**

slow   not fast [The baby liked the slow ride in the wagon.] —**slower, slowest**

small   little [The grapes were small.] —**smaller, smallest**

slide

smile   to show that one is happy [The gift made Maria smile.] —**smiles**

snail   a soft, slow-moving animal that lives in a spiral shell [A snail can live on land or in the water.] —**snails**

snow   soft, white flakes that fall from the sky in cold weather [Ken likes to ride a sled in the snow.]

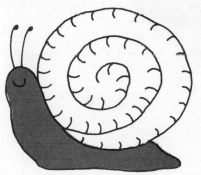

soap   a thing that makes suds to wash with [Lou cleaned her hands with soap and water.] —**soaps**

snail

south   direction toward the left when you face the sunset [Many birds fly south in the fall.]

speak   to talk [They speak to each other on the phone.] —**speaks, spoke, speaking**

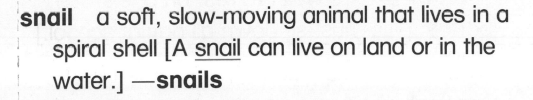

spoon

star

spoon   a tool for eating or stirring [Fred ate soup with a <u>spoon</u>.] —**spoons**

spot   a small mark [Missy has a <u>spot</u> of mud on her sock.] —**spots**

stand   to be or get on one's feet [<u>Stand</u> by your desk.] —**stands, stood, standing**

star   **I** a small, bright light in the night sky [That bright <u>star</u> is very far away.] **2** a shape with five points [Miss Jones put a gold <u>star</u> on my paper.] —**stars**

stay   to not move from one place [Ken had to <u>stay</u> in bed when he was sick.] —**stays, stayed, staying**

step   to move the foot [Take one <u>step</u> backward.] —**steps**

stick   a twig or branch [Linda used a small <u>stick</u> to draw in the sand.] —**sticks**

stop   to quit moving [The bus will <u>stop</u> to let the man off.] —**stops, stopped, stopping**

subway   an underground electric railway [Dad rides the <u>subway</u> to work.] —**subways**

summer   a time of the year after spring [We like to swim in the <u>summer</u>.]

sun   a large body in the sky that gives us light and heat [The <u>sun</u> shines during the day.]

sunny   bright from the sun [It can get hot on <u>sunny</u> days.] —**sunnier, sunniest**

surf   the white foam of waves [It is fun to float on the <u>surf</u>.]

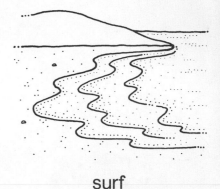

surf

---

tadpole   a young frog [The <u>tadpole</u> has a tail.] —**tadpoles**

tag   a chasing game [Chad chased me when we played <u>tag</u>.]

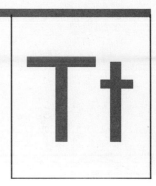

take   to get [I will <u>take</u> a turn if you let me.] —**takes, took, taking**

tame   no longer wild [Andrea has a <u>tame</u> rabbit for a pet.]

teach   to show or help to learn how to do something [Mom is going to <u>teach</u> me how to play chess.] —**teaches, taught, teaching**

tadpole

ten   the number after nine [I have <u>ten</u> toes.]

thank   to say to someone you like the kindness they did for you [I will <u>thank</u> Grandma for the gift.] —**thanks, thanked, thanking**

they   persons or animals being talked about [Chris and Joe said <u>they</u> missed the bus.]

this   a thing being talked about [<u>This</u> food tastes good.]

three   the number after two [A clover has <u>three</u> leaves.]

time   minutes, hours, days, and years [It took a long <u>time</u> to learn to tie my shoes.]

toad

toad   an animal like a frog that lives on land [A <u>toad</u> hopped out of the garden.] —**toads**

toe   one of the five parts at the end of the foot [Tess stepped on my big <u>toe</u>.] —**toes**

tooth   a bony, white part of the mouth used to bite and chew [Amy brushes each <u>tooth</u> carefully.] —**teeth**

top¹   the highest part [David went to the <u>top</u> of the hill.]

top

top²   a child's toy that spins [Carrie made the <u>top</u> spin.] —**tops**

train   a line of railroad cars [We took a <u>train</u> to see my aunt.] —**trains**

trap   a tool for catching animals [The mouse was in the <u>trap</u>.] —**traps**

tree   a large plant with branches and leaves [Wood comes from the trunk of a <u>tree</u>.] —**trees**

trunk   I the main part of a tree [The bark on the tree's <u>trunk</u> was smooth.] **2** an elephant's nose [The elephant picked up a nut with his <u>trunk</u>.] —**trunks**

try   to work on [Bill will <u>try</u> to pick up the heavy log.] —**tries, tried, trying**

tub   a thing that holds water for a bath [Ali washed the baby in the <u>tub</u>.] —**tubs**

turn   to move around a center point [The wheels of the car <u>turn</u>.] —**turns, turned, turning**

turtle

turtle   an animal with a hard shell, four legs, and a tail [A <u>turtle</u> can live on land or in water.] —**turtles**

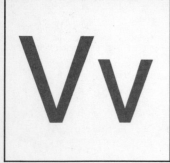

us   you and me [Dad took <u>us</u> to the park.]

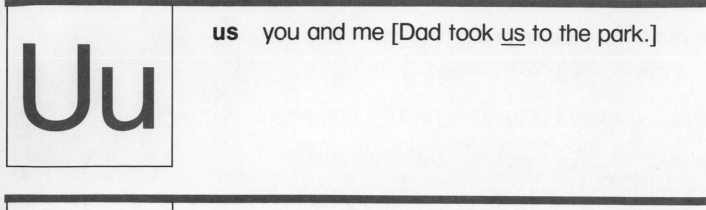

van   a closed truck [We took our bikes in the back of the <u>van</u>.] —**vans**

very   a big amount [I am <u>very</u> hungry.]

vest   a short garment without sleeves [Marcos wore a <u>vest</u> under his jacket.] —**vests**

vine   any plant with a long, thin stem that grows along the ground or climbs walls or trees, by fastening itself to them [The ivy <u>vine</u> grew up the walls.] —**vines**

wait   to stay in place or do nothing [<u>Wait</u> for the bell.] —**waits, waited, waiting**

wall   the flat side of a room [We hung a painting on the <u>wall</u>.] —**walls**

want   to wish for [Lin and Sherry <u>want</u> a new bike.] —**wants, wanted, wanting**

watch to look at [We <u>watch</u> the parade.]
—**watches, watched, watching**

we you and I [<u>We</u> want to eat lunch.]

weed a plant that grows where it is not
wanted [David pulled the ugly <u>weed</u> out of
his garden.] —**weeds**

went to be gone [We <u>went</u> to visit Carla.]

west

west toward the point where the sun sets [We
saw the sun set in the <u>west</u>.]

wet not dry [Water dripped from the <u>wet</u> rag.]
—**wetter, wettest**

wheel a round disk or frame that turns [I bent
the front <u>wheel</u> on my bike.] —**wheels**

when at what time? [<u>When</u> did you eat
lunch?]

where at what place? [<u>Where</u> are my
glasses?]

whisper to speak in a low, soft voice [<u>Whisper</u>
the secret to me.] —**whispers, whispered,
whispering**

white the color of clean snow or milk [The
bride wore a <u>white</u> dress.] —**whiter, whitest**

why   for what reason? [Why did Bob go home?]

will   a word that shows something is yet to be done [Pam will leave soon.]

win   to get by work or skill [Brian wants to win the prize.] —**wins, won, winning**

with   **1** in the care of [I went to the show with my mom.] **2** into [Mix blue with yellow to get green.] **3** having [The girl with the red coat is my friend.]

yes   the opposite of NO [Yes, I will eat my dinner.]

you   the person or persons talked to [You are my best friend.]

zebra   a wild animal of Africa that has dark stripes on a white or tan body [We saw a zebra in the zoo.] —**zebras**

zip   to join with a zipper [Neil will zip his coat to keep warm.] —**zips, zipped, zipping**

zoo   a place to see wild animals [The tigers at the zoo are kept in cages.] —**zoos**

My Spelling Notebook

My Spelling Notebook

My Spelling Notebook

My Spelling Notebook